FINLAND

Tan Chung Lee

MARSHALL CAVENDISH
New York • London • Sydney

Reference edition published 1996 by
Marshall Cavendish Corporation
99 White Plains Road
P.O. Box 2001
Tarrytown
New York 10591

© Times Editions Pte Ltd 1996

Originated and designed by
Times Books International, an imprint of
Times Editions Pte Ltd

Printed in Singapore

Library of Congress Cataloging-in-Publication Data:
Tan Chung Lee, 1949-
    Finland / Tan Chung Lee.
      p. cm.—(Cultures Of The World)
    Includes bibliographical references and index.
    Summary: Describes the geography, history, government,
people, and culture of this isolated country, which gained its
independence from Russia in 1917.
    ISBN 0-7614-0280-2 (lib. bdg.)
    1. Finland—Juvenile literature. [1. Finland.]
I. Title. II. Series.
DL1012.L44 1996
984.97—dc20   95–44860
            CIP
            AC

INTRODUCTION

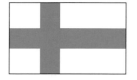 FINLAND'S ISOLATION has played an important role in shaping its history as a nation. From the air, it looks idyllic—miles of pine forests interspersed with thousands of lakes, the shores dotted with log cabins that are the summer homes of many Finnish families. But this placid scenery was, until recently, just a veneer. Beneath it all lay the story of a once troubled people who, for centuries, simply sought to survive on an infertile land with an inhospitable climate.

Finland was part of the Swedish kingdom from the Middle Ages until 1809, when it became part of the Russian empire. Few people thought that the country could ever gain its independence. Yet it did—in 1917. What is more, it has since grown into a modern, industrial nation renowned for its design talents. Today the people of Finland enjoy one of the highest standards of living in the world.

CONTENTS

Couple relaxing on a park bench, enjoying a summer afternoon.

CONTENTS

Reindeer crossing sign in Lapland.

GEOGRAPHY

FINLAND IS THE WORLD'S MOST NORTHERLY country with one quarter of its total land mass of 130,558 square miles (338,144 square kilometers) lying north of the Arctic Circle. Although it is the fifth largest country in Europe (about the size of New England, New York, and New Jersey combined) it is also one of the least populous, with five million people.

The entire country stretches 720 miles (1,160 kilometers) from north to south, and 335 miles (540 kilometers) from east to west. Except for a 680-mile-long (1,100-kilometer) coastline, the rest of Finland's 2,240-mile (3,600-kilometer) frontier is shared with other countries: Sweden to the west, Norway to the north, and the Russian Federation to the east.

Much of Finland is a low-lying plain. About 70% of the land area is forested. Only 8% is cultivated land, and the rest is wasteland made up of swamps, arctic fells, and sand.

Highlands are found only in Lapland, where the highest point is Haltiatunturi at 4,343 feet (1,324 meters).

TOPOGRAPHY AND LANDSCAPE

The bedrock underlying Finland is among the world's oldest. Much of the country's physical features were formed during the last Ice Age millions of years ago. The continental glacier carved out the lake basins that lie in a northwest to southeast direction, and when it stopped, it left behind on its rim the Salpausselkä Ridge, which lies south of the Lake District. In fact, the swift-running currents of the melting glacier formed several ridges, known as eskers, that run parallel to the lake basins. The lake-encircled ridges near the city of Savonlinna in Finland's Lake District are a prime example.

Because of the disappearance of the continental glacier, the country's land mass is still rising. The land along the Gulf of Finland, for example, rises 12 inches (30 centimeters) every 100 years, while on the Gulf of Bothnia it goes up by as much as 36 inches (90 centimeters). It is estimated that the total land mass increases by 2.7 square miles (7 square kilometers) each year. Much of the land along the coasts is low-lying plains. Inland there are mounds and hills interspersed with lakes and rivers.

Finland is such a long country that the landscape from south to north varies greatly; the gently rolling rural landscape in the south gradually gives way to hills and huge forested areas in the north. The only mountainous area in the country is in the northwest, near Norway, where peaks rise to just over 3,300 feet (1,000 meters).

Two-thirds of Finland is covered with forest. It has more forest area per capita than any other country in Europe with 9.8 acres (4 hectares) of forest per person. Finland's 188,000 lakes provide 121 feet (37 meters) of lakeside per person. Wild animals such as elk, bears, and occasionally wolves roam the forests of spruce, birch, and pine. In the foothills of Lapland, reindeer herds wander freely.

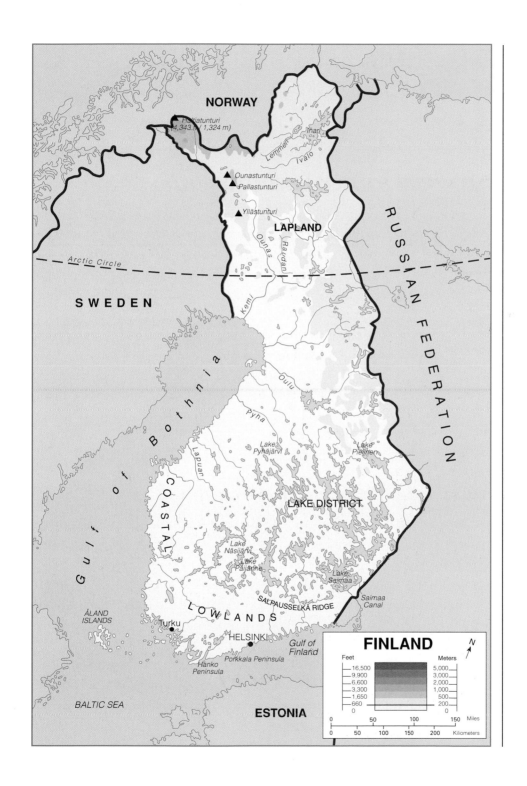

NORWAY

Haltiatunturi
(4,343 ft / 1,324 m)

Inari

Lemmen

Ivalo

▲ Ounastunturi

▲ Pallastunturi

▲ Yllästunturi

LAPLAND

Ounas

Raudan

Arctic Circle

RUSSIAN FEDERATION

SWEDEN

Kemi

Oulu

Pyha

Lake
Pyhäjärvi

Lake
Pielinen

Gulf of Bothnia

Lapuan

LAKE DISTRICT

COASTAL

Lake
Näsijärvi

Lake
Päijänne

Lake
Saimaa

Saimaa
Canal

ÅLAND
ISLANDS

LOWLANDS

SALPAUSSELKÄ RIDGE

Turku

HELSINKI

Gulf of
Finland

Porkkala Peninsula

Hänko
Peninsula

BALTIC SEA

ESTONIA

FINLAND

Feet		Meters
16,500		5,000
9,900		3,000
6,600		2,000
3,300		1,000
1,650		500
660		200
0		0

0	50	100	150	Miles

0	50	100	150	200	Kiliometers

9

In the Lake District, many of the lakes are connected by short rivers and channels, making it easier for people to get around by boat.

THE COAST AND ARCHIPELAGO

Southwest Finland along the coast is one of the country's most beautiful areas and its most historical. The main centers are Helsinki, the capital, and Turku, the former capital, noted for its medieval castle and cathedral. In the west the Gulf of Bothnia, an arm of the Baltic Sea, forms a natural barrier between Sweden and Finland, while in the south the Gulf of Finland separates the country from the Baltic states of Estonia, Latvia, and Lithuania.

A look at a map of Finland shows an archipelago of 17,000 tree-covered islands and smaller skerries (small, rocky islands, or reefs) scattered off its coast, extending right up to the Åland Islands. The waters around this scenic archipelago are a yachtsman's paradise.

THE LAKE DISTRICT

Finland has more lakes than any other country, with 22 over 75 square miles (200 square kilometers) in size. The biggest lake is Lake Saimaa at 443 square miles (1,147 square kilometers), which with other lakes forms the Saimaa Lake System.

The beautiful lakelands are at the heart of Finland, occupying almost a third of the whole country. Thousands of lakes flow down the many rivers to drain into the Baltic Sea. Before the days of roads and railways, the lakes formed narrow waterways linking towns across central Finland. Ships were the only means of travel then. Although you can travel in the area by road today, following the natural contours of the lake, it is still possible to sail in a passenger ship.

LAPLAND—LAND OF THE MIDNIGHT SUN

Covering the extreme north of Finland and located almost entirely above the Arctic Circle, Lapland is the land of the midnight sun. From mid-May, for 70 days and nights, the sun never dips below the horizon. Then there is a 50-day "sunset" when the sky gets dark, followed by the sunless days of *kaamos* ("KAAH-mos") when it is nighttime even at noon—a period that lasts nearly six months. This is the season of the spectacular northern lights, which dance across the arctic sky, setting it ablaze with shafts of colored light.

Many people visit Lapland to see the midnight sun or to experience *kaamos* in winter. But its great wilderness is also a big attraction. Lapland, which occupies one-third of the land mass of Finland, has plenty of open space and herds of roaming reindeer. Unlike the rest of Finland, there are few lakes in Lapland but many rivers separated by vast stretches of uninhabited land. Lots of pine and spruce can be found in the valleys. Above the valleys are fells, gently rounded hills that are the result of the erosion of glaciers around gorges. The fells are treeless except for occasional scrub.

At the height of summer, the sun can be seen even at night, giving the phenomenon the appropriate name of "midnight sun."

WHEN TO SEE THE MIDNIGHT SUN

Visitors to Finland are assured of seeing the midnight sun if they are in the country between May 17 and June 25. At the peak of summer in northern Finland, the sun is above the horizon 24 hours a day. In Utsjoki, the longest summer day occurs over a two-month period. Even in southern Finland, there is no complete darkness during the nights—the long evening twilight merges with an equally long morning dawn.

HELSINKI

Helsinki's Market Square, located next to the harbor, is distinguished by the surrounding neoclassical buildings and the bustling activity at its many fruit, flower, vegetable, and fish stalls.

Helsinki became the capital of Finland in 1812, replacing Turku. It has a unique character, as it bears the stamp of both its Swedish and Russian heritage. Founded in 1550, Helsinki was known as Helsingfors in Swedish. In 1748 the Swedes built the sea-castle on the island of Suomenlinna, just outside the city. Yet there is also much about Helsinki that reminds the visitor of the time when it was a Grand Duchy of Russia, particularly the magnificent Senate Square with its Lutheran Cathedral and surrounding buildings. The Orthodox Uspenski Cathedral with its gilded onion domes and the city's many Russian restaurants add to Helsinki's tsarist flavor. Architecturally, it bears such a great resemblance to tsarist St. Petersburg that several U.S. movies with a Russian setting have been shot on location in Helsinki instead of Russia.

The city also has many modern buildings, and its parks and proximity to the sea give it an attractive setting. With a population of only half a million, it is uncongested, with many open spaces.

TAMPERE

Tampere, Finland's second largest city with a population of about 175,000, enjoys a beautiful setting between the lakes of Näsijärvi and Pyhäjärvi in southwest Finland. In the past, it was a manufacturing center, as its location on the water's edge made it the perfect setting for industries. Today many of the factories are being renovated for use as cultural centers, and Tampere is becoming a leisure and cultural city. The Tampere Biennale of new Finnish music was held for the fifth time in April 1994.

Even though Tampere is an important inland urban center with many cultural attractions, nature is never far away. There are about 180 lakes within the city's borders.

TURKU

Turku is Finland's oldest—and third largest—city and main port with a population of 160,000. It was a thriving trading center as early as the 13th century and served as the capital of Finland until 1812. The city thus offers many historical sights. The famous medieval Turku Castle is the main attraction. Now used as a museum, it was Sweden's major defensive position in Finland during the Middle Ages and survived several battles and sieges.

Another medieval attraction, Turku Cathedral, took two centuries to complete after building started in the 13th century. Many well-known figures in Finnish history are buried in the main cathedral and its side chapels. Offshore, the scenic beauty can best be appreciated by taking a cruise and sailing among its many islands.

Above: **During the winter, birds depend on their feathers to protect them against the extreme cold, and their resting spots are carefully chosen not only to provide shelter, but also to catch whatever warmth the sun may provide.**

Opposite (top): **There are about 400–600 bears left in Finland today, and bear hunting is strictly regulated. Finland has a good record in animal conservation.**

Opposite (bottom): **Although reindeer used to wander freely across the north of Scandinavia, today they are half tame, spending the winter in farm courtyards.**

CLIMATE

Despite its northerly location, Finland has a milder climate than expected, thanks to the Baltic Sea, the island waters, and the westerly winds from the Atlantic, which are warmed by the Gulf Stream. The country enjoys an annual average temperature that is 43°F (6°C) warmer than other countries on the same latitude. However, east and southeast winds from the Eurasian continent bring heat waves in summer and cold spells in winter.

There are regional differences in the climate as well as variations in the seasons. Winter is a long season in the north, with snow arriving as early as October and lasting until late April in Lapland. In the south, the first snow falls in December and the days are short, lasting under six hours. The average winter temperature in the south is 26°F (-3°C).

Summers in Finland are warm. In the south, the temperature in July averages 68°F (20°C), although it can go up to 86°F (30°C) during the day. The south also receives 8 inches (20 cm) more rain than in the north; on the average, the country has about 100 days of rain each year.

FINLAND'S LEGENDARY ICEBREAKERS

Finnish winters are long and severe, freezing the Gulf of Bothnia and Gulf of Finland for months each year. However, Finland's harbors do not remain frozen for long thanks to the hardworking fleet of Finnish icebreakers, which ranks as one of the world's most efficient. More than half of the world's icebreakers are built in Finland.

Finnish icebreakers are used in the Arctic and the Antarctic to open up icy passages. So magnificent is the experience aboard an icebreaker that icebreaker cruises are offered to tourists. Conducted between December and May, the cruises take place in the northern Gulf of Bothnia, home of Europe's largest continuous ice field, located at the same latitude as Alaska.

FLORA AND FAUNA

Finland lies in the northern coniferous forest zone, and its flora and fauna are typical of this zone. The most common natural vegetation is forest; the trees that grow are mainly birch, pine, and spruce. Oak is found in the extreme south and southwest. The country also has substantial areas of swampland.

Animals include the wolf, bear, lynx, and wolverine, while elk, reindeer, Saimaa seals, beavers, and white-tailed and Finnish deer are also abundant. Some animals, such as elk, are so numerous that hunting is allowed to keep them in check.

There are at least 60 different species of mammals; those found in the forests are the fox, squirrel, and hare. There are more than 350 bird species, most of them migratory. Native bird species include the blackbird, white-tailed eagle, osprey, and eagle. The white-tailed eagle was once considered an endangered species but is now increasing in number.

Fish is plentiful and over 70 species exist. The commercially important ones are the Baltic herring and whitefish. Reptiles and frogs are less common, with 11 species found. The most common snake is the viper.

HISTORY

FINLAND DATES ITS HISTORY from the end of the last Ice Age 40,000 years ago, when the continental glacier melted and land rose from the sea. The first settlers who moved into the area of forests and lakes between the Gulf of Finland, the Gulf of Bothnia, and Lake Ladoga were said to belong to the Finno-Ugrian group of people. It was only much later that they were joined by the Finns, who gave the country its name, migrating from the southern parts of the Gulf of Finland. About 2,000 years ago, migrants from the Baltic areas added to the mix.

Above: **This Stone Age mace in the shape of an elk's head was found in Finland.**

Opposite: **Olavinlinna Castle in Savonlinna, begun in 1475 during the period of Swedish control.**

There are indications that the upper part of Finland down to the Arctic Circle was occupied during the Stone Age (7500–1500 B.C.), mainly along the coast. Later, during the Bronze Age (1500–500 B.C.) and Iron Age (500 B.C.–400 A.D.), the settlers moved inland, developing trade and cultural ties with the west and east. During the Viking period, close links with Scandinavia and Russia were forged. The Vikings raided far and wide, working westwards from Scandinavia and to the east as far as Constantinople. Their route took them through the Lake Mälaren valley and the Götaland region in Sweden, and southwards across the Gulf of Finland.

Records of the Viking expeditions started from the year 800. Their campaigns into Russia and Byzantium continued well into the 10th and 11th centuries and were said to have also involved the participation of some Finns. When the Scandinavians converted to Christianity and ended their marauding on distant territories, the Finnish and Baltic pagans continued their exploits, and these are recounted in the epic *Kalevala* tales.

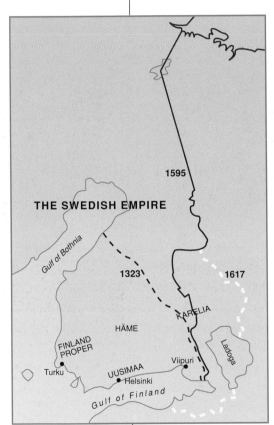

THE SWEDISH EMPIRE

1595

1323

1617

Gulf of Bothnia

HÄME

KARELIA

Ladoga

FINLAND PROPER

Turku

UUSIMAA

Helsinki

Viipuri

Gulf of Finland

Changes in Finland's eastern frontiers between 1323 and 1617.

THE SWEDISH PERIOD (1200–1809)

Finland as we know it today was rather fragmented until about the 13th century. It loosely included different areas dominated by three main tribes that were hostile toward one another: the Finns, the Tavastians, and the Karelians. The Finns in the southwest and Häme had links with the West and the Karelians were oriented toward the East, while part of western Finland, the archipelago, and the Åland Islands had once been part of the Central Swedish military and economic system. This lack of unity in Finland attracted the interest of its neighbors, who sought to gain political control: Sweden in the west under the influence of the Roman Catholic Church, and the Russian city of Novgorod in the east backed by the Greek Orthodox Church.

The new Swedish kingdom tried to reestablish its old ties with Finland. The first crusade, led by King Eric and St. Henry, the Bishop of Uppsala (in Sweden), was launched to increase Swedish influence. Missionaries conducted their work around Turku and the inner areas around Tampere. Christianity was firmly established in southwestern Finland in the mid-12th century. After the Pope gave his sanction in 1216, the Swedes continued their quest with a second crusade into Tavastia. They entered Häme, Uusimaa, and Karelia, where they built a castle. Soon, Swedish immigrants moved in to settle along the coast. In the meantime, Novgorod was trying to extend its influence along the Gulf of Finland and the area around Lake

Ladoga, while Denmark and Germany were gaining control of the coastal regions along the old eastern route.

While Novgorod was fighting off the Mongolians, the Swedes tried to move east from Finland to the River Neva but were defeated in 1240. Sweden and Novgorod continued their battle for the control of Finland and the eastern coast of the Gulf of Finland well into the third crusade in 1293, when Sweden built the Wiborg fortress and city. In 1300, they established a fort on the banks of the River Neva but this was destroyed by Novgorod.

The war finally ended in 1343 with the Treaty of Pähkinäsaari, which established the border between Sweden and Novgorod for the first time. The eastern part of Karelia was made part of Novgorod, linking it to Russia and the Orthodox Church. All areas west of the border, including western Karelia and south Finland, came under the Swedish kingdom and the Roman Catholic Church. The new border thus divided the people of Karelia between two kingdoms, religions, and cultures.

Under Sweden, Swedish law and the Scandinavian social system were established. The Finns enjoyed full political rights. In 1362, they were given the right to participate in the elections of the king through the Finnish body of *lagman* ("LAG-mern"), now known as *Eduskuntar* ("ED-oos-koon-tah"). In the 16th century, a legislative assembly representing four groups—the nobility, clergy, burghers, and farmers—was set up, known as the Diet of the Four Estates.

Turku Castle was constructed in the 13th century. The seat of power during the Swedish period was in Turku, which also became the episcopal see with the appointment of the first Finnish bishop, Maunu I, in 1291.

THE GREAT POWER PERIOD (1617–1721)

Sweden's Great Power period from 1617 to 1721 began with the reign of Gustavus II Adolphus when the Swedes began their expansionist policy targeting the Baltic countries, Poland, and Germany. As the Baltic region gradually came under Swedish control, the border of Finland was pushed farther east. Apart from suffering military action in the area, the Finns were also conscripted into battle.

Another development during this period was the process of "Swedification" in Finland. There was a tightening of administrative control in all aspects of Finnish life to ensure uniformity with Stockholm, Sweden's capital city and its administrative, economic, and cultural hub. The highest posts were filled by Swedes and the Swedish language grew in importance in Finland.

RUSSIAN OCCUPATION

Russia, in the meantime, began to expand westwards, encroaching upon Finland and other Swedish-occupied territory. From 1710 to 1714, Russia took over the whole of Finland as far as the Åland Islands. The occupation period, known as the Great Wrath, ended in 1721. Although Sweden regained control of Finland, it lost Karelia in southeast Finland to the Russians. Another war, known as the War of the Hats, broke out between 1741 and 1743. Russia occupied Finland yet again during a period known as the Lesser Wrath. Under the Peace of Turku in 1743, Russia agreed to

A war memorial in Hanko stands as a lonely reminder of the struggle with Russia for control of Finland. Finland's importance to Russia lay in its strategic location near St. Petersburg, Russia's western capital. By controlling the Gulf of Finland, Russia could prevent enemy attacks.

withdraw its troops in return for more territory, pushing the border farther westward. Sweden ceded to Russia the fortified towns of Hamina and Lappeenranta in southeast Finland and the Olavinlinna fortress.

There were feelings in some quarters that Finland should separate from Sweden. Finnish representatives in the Diet at Stockholm demanded special aid to compensate for what their country had suffered during the periods of Russian occupation. This resulted in the introduction of

Uspenski Cathedral in Helsinki shows the Russian influence on Finnish culture.

economic reforms and a boosting of Finnish defense over the next few decades. Trade restrictions were removed, a fortress on Suomenlinna was built, and a strong coastal naval fleet was developed. Living standards improved, especially during the reign of Gustavus III (1771–1792), and new towns were established. Finnish literature developed. The Finnish language was accepted in the Diet and for use on currency, and more Finns were appointed to the civil service.

From 1788 to 1790, there was another war with Russia. A move among some military officers to try to separate Finland from Sweden found little support. However, this secessionist attempt was to influence Russia's actions in a war from 1808 to 1809 when, instead of returning occupied territory to Sweden, the Russians held on to Finland, making it a buffer zone with its own Diet and administration.

Tsar Alexander I, Grand Duke of Finland, addressing the Finnish Assembly at the opening ceremony of the Diet in Porvoo in 1809, held at the city's cathedral. The oil painting by Emanuel Thelning was completed between 1809 and 1812.

FINLAND AS AN AUTONOMOUS GRAND DUCHY

The tsar of Russia, Alexander I, personally supervised the affairs of Finland. The Finns had already pledged their loyalty to the tsar in a session of the Finnish Diet held in Porvoo in 1809. In return for their allegiance, the tsar promised that he would let them continue practicing their own Evangelical Lutheran faith, and that they would have equal constitutional laws and rights. In effect, Finland became an autonomous Grand Duchy with its own institutions—a sort of separate state within Russia. The tsar was the constitutional monarch and was represented by a governor-general. The highest government body was the Senate, made up of Finns who still maintained their Diet of the Four Estates. The Finns also had their own representative at the court of St. Petersburg, who could personally present to the tsar matters concerning Finland.

To weaken the influence of Sweden, the tsar encouraged building and development in Finland, and Helsinki was made the new capital. The system of roads and canals was improved. Elegant buildings went up to beautify the city.

The period of autonomy gave rise to a new Finnish national consciousness. Finnish literature developed and a movement for a language-based political party grew. During the reigns of Alexander III (1881–1894) and Nicholas II (1894–1917), questions were raised about Finland's autonomous status by the extremist Pan-Slavist group in Russia. Objections to Finnish autonomy resulted in the February Manifesto of 1899, which diminished the authority of the Finnish Diet. There was a protest movement among the Finns, but it failed to have any effect. The Finns were divided no longer by language but by their outlook on Russia.

Constitutionalists combined with Social Democrats to lead the Great Strike of 1905. Here Finns gather on Senate Square, singing the National Anthem in protest after Russia's defeat in the Russo-Japanese War.

The Russo-Japanese War in 1904–05, in which Russia was defeated, resulted in a general strike that extended into Finland, forcing the tsar to liberalize his rule. This led to a radical parliamentary reform in Finland in 1906 with a new single-chamber parliament replacing the Four Estates Diet. Thus overnight Finland switched from the oldest parliamentary system to the most modern. Universal suffrage was introduced, and the right to vote was extended to women—a first in Europe.

However, this did not prevent another wave of oppression from 1908 to 1914, resulting in the "Russification" of the Senate. Finland's autonomy was restored during the Russian Revolution of 1917. Later in the same year, Finland managed to break completely free from Russian rule.

General Carl Gustaf Mannerheim led his White camp to victory in the civil war that broke out after the declaration of independence.

INDEPENDENT FINLAND

The chaos of the October 1917 revolution in Russia gave Finland a chance to break free. On December 6, 1917, the Senate, under P.E. Svinhufvud, declared Finland an independent republic. Despite independence, Soviet troops remained in Finland, which was then divided into Red and White camps. The Socialists, or Reds, who were anxious to retain Russian ties, gained control of the Social Democratic Party and introduced their own Russian-style revolution at the end of January 1918. Taking over Helsinki and south Finland, they forced the Senate to flee to Vaasa in Ostrobothnia, where a White government was set up, controlling northern and central Finland.

In the civil war that erupted, the Whites received assistance from imperial Germany, with which they had close ties, while the Reds had help from Russia. In May 1918, the Whites, under General Carl Gustaf Mannerheim, won a major battle in Tampere that ended the civil war. Russia pulled out its troops from Finland. Germany then tried to move in to establish its sphere of influence firmly.

However, Mannerheim did not favor strong German links and moved to forge ties with the Allied forces instead. Mannerheim, who became Finland's head of state and held the title of "Regent," also ratified the constitution on July 17, 1919, and Great Britain and the United States finally recognized Finnish independence. K.J. Ståhlberg was elected the first president of the Finnish republic that same

year. In 1920, Finland and Russia normalized relations by signing the Peace of Tartu.

The Finnish constitution was a compromise between the republican and the monarchist camps. It gave the president much of the power wielded by the head of state under the previous constitution. Responsible for foreign policy, he was also made commander-in-chief of the armed forces and had the power to dissolve parliament. The Finnish parliament was kept busy passing legislation in the first years of the new republic. Laws were passed introducing compulsory education and military service, freedom of speech and worship, freedom to form societies, land reform, and the prohibition of alcohol (repealed in 1932).

There was a period of healing when Ståhlberg passed an amnesty act that granted pardon to those convicted of leading the Reds. The civil war wounds were further eased when the Social Democratic Party was allowed

The statue of K.J. Ståhlberg, the first president of Finland, stands outside Parliament House in Helsinki.

to take part in elections in 1919; it later became the largest party in parliament. In 1926–27, the Social Democrats went on to form the government. In 1929, the anti-communist Lapua movement was born, patterned after the Italian Fascists, a group that encouraged militarism and nationalism. The Lapua movement—which had wide support among peasants who had suffered greatly during the worldwide Great Depression—carried out an armed revolt in 1932, but it was squashed and later outlawed.

Finnish foreign policy at the outset was guided by the directions of the League of Nations. However, when the latter was unable to maintain world peace, Finland announced in 1935 that its security issues would be oriented towards Scandinavia. In the meantime, the Soviet Union, anxious to bolster the defense of Leningrad, was demanding that Finland give up some of its territory and allow a Soviet base to be built on the Hanko peninsula. Finland refused. In August 1939, the Soviet Union and Germany secretly signed a Non-Aggression Pact that ensured German neutrality when the Soviet Union attacked Finland later in November.

Although Finland was ill-equipped and fought alone in the Winter War that ensued, it managed to survive for three-and-a-half months.

The war ended with the Peace of Moscow, signed in March 1940. Finland gave up the Karelian Isthmus and the outer islands of the Gulf of Finland to the Soviets, who acquired a base on Hanko. Still, Finnish fears of Soviet intervention continued and grew worse when the Baltic states were forcibly made part of the Soviet Union in August 1940.

By then, Soviet-German relations were starting to strain. Isolated from the West and with Sweden remaining neutral, Finland leaned towards Germany. So when Adolf Hitler invaded the Soviet Union in June 1941, the Finns followed suit with what became known as the Continuation War.

Finland occupied Eastern Karelia on the other side of the border with plans to annex it. The Finns thought that if they remained neutral, the country would be occupied by either the Germans or Soviets. However, there was no alliance with Germany, although it had troops in northern Finland, and the Finns did not take part in the siege of Leningrad.

The Soviets launched a massive counterattack. In spring, Helsinki was bombed and heavy fighting broke out on the isthmus. Finland withdrew from the war a year before Germany fell. In September 1944, an armistice was declared in Moscow with terms dictated by the Soviets. Finland returned to its 1940 border in Eastern Karelia and, in place of Hanko, the

Finnish soldiers during the Winter War of 1939-1940. In the Winter War, the Russians attacked with large tanks, which got stuck in ditches or were blown up with explosives, while the Finns fought on skis with white uniforms as camouflage.

As Finland's president, Urho Kekkonen continued his country's policy of neutrality. This suited the interests of the Soviet Union, which openly backed his reelection in 1962.

Porkkala Peninsula was leased to the Soviets for 50 years. Finland also agreed to pay war damages and reduce the size of its army. German troops in Lapland refused to leave and the Finns had to force them out in a bitter battle that ended in the spring of 1945.

Finland suffered greatly from the Continuation War with 65,000 dead and 158,000 wounded. Homes had to be found for 423,000 Eastern Karelians who chose to cross over the border to Finland rather than stay under Soviet rule. The new president, Juho K. Paasikivi, who succeeded Mannerheim in 1946, pursued a policy of reconciliation with the Soviet Union.

In 1948, Finland signed a Treaty of Friendship, Cooperation, and Mutual Assistance with Moscow by which it agreed to prevent any attack on the Soviet Union through Finnish territory. Finland's aim to remain outside great power conflicts became the cornerstone of the Paasikivi line in foreign policy.

Over the years, Finnish external relations began to stabilize. Finland paid off its war debt on time, the only one among countries involved in World War II to do so. As payment was in the form of industrial goods, Finland had to reorganize its production structure. Machinery was rebuilt and the process of industrialization speeded up. This paid off in the long run as it resulted in rapid economic development of the country. Finland completed its war payments in 1952, the same year that Helsinki hosted the Olympic Games.

In 1955, the Soviets ended their 50-year lease of Porkkala and returned it to Finland. The same year, Finland was accepted into the United Nations

Danemark
Espagne
Finlande
Président
France
Grande-Bretagne
Grèce
Hongrie
Irlande

and the Nordic Council. In 1956, Urho Kekkonen became president and actively pursued Finland's policy of neutrality. In 1961, the country became an associate member of the European Free Trade Association (EFTA) and in 1973 signed a free-trade agreement with the European Economic Commission (later renamed the European Union, or EU). In 1993, it joined the European Economic Area (EEA) and started negotiations to join the EU, of which it became a member together with Austria and Sweden on January 1, 1995.

In 1975, Finland's neutral position was boosted when it hosted the Conference on Security and Cooperation in Europe (CSCE). Kekkonen resigned as president in 1981 for reasons of ill health. He was succeeded by Mauno Koivisto, who was elected in 1982. In 1992, Finland again hosted the follow-up CSCE summit. By then, the world was changing rapidly as the Soviet Union had broken up the previous year.

GOVERNMENT

FINLAND IS RELATIVELY YOUNG as an independent nation. For 700 years, from the Middle Ages until 1809, it was part of the Swedish kingdom. It was considered the eastern part of the realm and its social, economic, legal, and administrative institutions were patterned after those in Sweden. After the 1808–1809 war with Russia, Finland was linked to the Russian empire. It was run as an autonomous Grand Duchy under the Russian tsar, who functioned as the Grand Duke. It was only on December 6, 1917, that Finland severed its ties with Russia and became a sovereign republican state.

THE CONSTITUTION

When Finland was an autonomous Grand Duchy, it had its own constitution and form of government. The Finnish constitution was ratified on July 17, 1919, and is still in force today. Basically, the constitution guarantees the rights of the citizens, who are considered equal before the law. Ultimate power is in the hands of the people, who are represented by parliament. In 1928, the Parliament Act was passed. It laid down the rules regarding the structure of parliament, its duties, and the electoral system.

There are 200 members of parliament and they are elected by a direct vote for a period for four years. However, the constitution gives the president of the Finnish republic the right to dissolve parliament before the end of four years and to declare fresh elections. There are 14 electoral districts from which members are elected to parliament. The autonomous Åland Islands are represented by one member.

The Finnish parliament works hand in hand with the president, who has the authority to initiate legislation and give his consent to laws. Parliament, on the other hand, oversees the work of the government and sanctions its budget proposals.

In contrast to the president, the prime minister has little independent authority, except the ability to swing the vote either way when there is a tie in parliament. Many of Finland's presidents have held the post of prime minister before assuming the presidency.

Opposite: **The presidential palace in Helsinki was built in 1818 as a private residence and redesigned in 1943 by C.L. Engel. Today it houses the presidential offices.**

RESULTS OF MARCH 1995 GENERAL ELECTION	
Name of Party	**Number of Parliamentary Seats Won**
Social Democratic Party	63
Finnish Center	44
National Coalition Party	39
Left-wing Alliance	22
Swedish People's Party	12
Greens	9
Christian League	7
Progressive Finnish Party	2
Rural Party	1
Ecological Party	1

A Social Democratic Party general election poster.

ROLE OF THE PRESIDENT

The constitution invests in the president very comprehensive powers. Those include the right to declare elections, call for emergency sittings of parliament, preside over its opening and closing, and even dissolve it. The president is responsible for foreign policy and is the commander-in-chief of the nation's armed forces. He is the one who decides on legislative proposals to parliament. He issues statutes, gives his consent to laws, or applies his temporary right of veto.

The president presides over the Council of State, or Cabinet, which stands by his decisions and through which he exercises his power. However, he usually attends only those Council of State meetings that are on matters within his power. All other meetings of the Council are held by the prime minister. The president is not obliged to take into consideration the views of the prime minister or the majority of the Council of State, but in practice he usually does.

PRESIDENTIAL ELECTIONS

Martti Ahtisaari, a former United Nations diplomat, was elected the 10th president of the Republic of Finland on February 6, 1994. It was the country's first presidential election by direct vote. Ahtisaari, who succeeded Mauno Koivisto, is a Social Democrat.

Nominations for presidential candidates are received from political parties with at least one member of parliament elected in earlier parliamentary elections. Also, anyone with proof of more than 20,000 supporters may run for election. In 1994, 11 presidential candidates ran for election.

Under Finland's electoral laws, if one candidate receives more than half the vote in the first election on January 16, he or she becomes the president. However, if no candidate receives more than half the vote, a second election is held on February 6 between the two candidates with the most votes in the first election. Ahtisaari's opponent in the second election in 1994 was Defense Minister Elisabeth Rehn of the Swedish People's Party.

All Finnish citizens aged 18 years and above have the right to vote. The elected president, who must be a native-born Finn, takes office on March 1 for a six-year term. The same president can only serve for two consecutive terms. The official residence of the president is Mantyniemi, the first presidential residence built for that purpose, completed in November 1993.

In 1907 Finland became the first country to elect women to parliament. That year saw 19 women seated in parliament, including feminist and former servant Miina Sillanpää, who would remain in office for 40 years.

The town hall in Turku, the old capital.

THE COUNCIL OF STATE

There are 12 ministries under the Council of State, headed by the prime minister. The prime minister and his ministers are appointed by the president, and they have to be native-born Finns.

Each ministry has its own area of responsibility and is headed by a minister. However, with some portfolios in certain ministries shared by two ministers, there are currently 17 ministers in the Council of State, plus the prime minister. The Council decides on important state affairs. Less significant issues are handled by the ministers. Many of the ministries have boards consisting of senior civil servants who meet regularly to deal with issues.

POLITICAL ADMINISTRATION

Administratively, Finland is divided into 12 provinces, each headed by a governor who is appointed by the president. Each province has a local government that is responsible for administration, law, and order, in its own area. Central and local government are kept separate and the country is divided into 460 municipalities, of which 94 are towns.

LOCAL GOVERNMENT

Provincial governments are given extensive powers under the constitution. They are responsible for the administration of their localities and for matters concerning hospitals, schools, social welfare, and town planning.

34

THE ÅLAND ISLANDS

The offshore Åland Islands enjoy a special position for historical reasons. Since 1856, at the time of the Crimean War, the islands were recognized in international law as an unfortified area. Most of its people are Swedish-speaking.

The islands have been largely autonomous since 1920, a status that was reaffirmed in 1951. A governor is the highest official. The islands also have a provincial parliament with 30 members who are chosen in a general election. The parliament has to give its approval to any change in, or repeal of, laws of a constitutional nature. A seven-member government body headed by the provincial president carries out the administration of the islands, the capital of which is Mariehamn.

Some funds for administration are provided for by the central government, although the provinces can levy taxes to raise money. In exchange for financial assistance, the central government retains control over the work of the local authorities. However, there are moves to increase the autonomy of the provinces.

The highest office in local government is the municipal council, which is a decision-making body. The members, numbering 17 to 85 depending on the size of the population of the municipality, are elected directly. The councils vote for their own chairman. Members of the executive committee—the municipal board—are also elected by the councils every two years. Administrative functions are carried out by statutory and voluntary committees appointed by the councils.

The municipal or town manager holds the highest office in local government. He is appointed by the municipal council and is answerable to the municipal board.

Celebrating Self Rule Day in the Åland Islands.

Defense Minister Elisabeth Rehn of the Social Democratic Party lost the presidential election to Martti Ahtisaari in 1994.

POLITICAL PARTIES

Nine parties had members elected to parliament during the last general election. The parties campaign actively in all kinds of elections—local, general, and presidential—and occupy administrative positions in which their members can exercise political power.

Since the end of World War II, the government has been made up of a coalition of different political parties. It started with the Agrarian Party (now the Finnish Center) forming a coalition government with the Social Democratic Party. In 1987, the Finnish Center was replaced by the opposition National Coalition Party, which formed a government with the Social Democratic Party. In 1991, the Finnish Center was back in power, this time forming a coalition with the National Coalition Party. But in the March 1995 general election, it was the Social Democratic Party that won the greatest number of parliamentary seats.

THE JUDICIARY

The constitution guarantees the independence of the judiciary, which appoints all judges to its courts.

There are three levels of courts in civil and criminal cases. The first is the circuit court, or city court, in the so-called "ancient cities." The Court of Appeal is next. Then comes the Supreme Court, which is the highest judicial authority. In the provinces, administrative cases are dealt with by the county administrative courts; appeal cases are heard in the Supreme Administrative Court. There are special courts to handle issues such as housing, land rights, and insurance.

Presidents and members of the Supreme Court and Supreme Administrative Court are appointed by the Finnish president on the recommendation of the courts. Judges of the circuit courts are appointed by the Supreme Court; the other members are nominated by municipal councils. The highest legal office is that of the Chancellor of Justice appointed by the president. The chancellor is also the highest public prosecutor overseeing the provincial police superintendents, sheriffs, and municipal public prosecutors. He sees to it that government authorities comply with the law and perform their duties. The chancellor attends the meetings of the Council of State and determines the legality of any decisions made.

Policemen in Mariehamn, capital of the Åland Islands.

ECONOMY

TRADITIONALLY, agriculture and forestry have been the root of Finland's economy. The country did not become an industrialized nation until well after the end of World War II. Payment of heavy war debts to the Soviet Union forced Finland to industrialize rapidly.

In 1950 as many as 46% of all Finnish workers were engaged in primary production, while the industrial and service sectors each had only 27% of the labor force. The situation changed in just over 20 years, as Finland became a highly developed industrial country in the 1970s. Real growth in its Gross Domestic Product (GDP) averaged 5% a year from 1950 to 1974. Although it slowed down after 1975, GDP growth surged again to nearly 6% in the boom years of the 1980s. The GDP went into a tailspin when the country entered a recession at the start of the 1990s. There were several reasons: overheating of the economy in the 1980s, lack of growth in the public sector in the 1970s and 1980s, an increased deficit in the country's balance of payments, central and local government indebtedness, and loss of its main trading partner when the Soviet Union collapsed.

The economic downturn resulted in a rise in unemployment and the value of the Finnish *markka* ("MAR-kah") plunged by a quarter when its ties with the European Community (EC) and the Exchange Mechanism System (EMS) were cut and it was allowed to float in the market.

Thanks to rapid industrialization, the Finns are able to enjoy a higher standard of living than many of their European neighbors. Per capita GDP in 1990 was one of the world's highest and the Finns' purchasing power was above average for Europe.

Opposite: **Logs are floated down rivers to their destinations. When logs become jammed at bends the lumberjack uses a long pole to free them.**

Above: **Finland's new bank notes were introduced in 1987. There are no restrictions on the sums of money that may be imported into or exported from Finland.**

A mobile saw mill is kept busy in a land where trees provide the raw material for many of the rural houses, as well as much of the furniture.

AGRICULTURE AND FORESTRY

Farmers in Finland have always combined agriculture with forestry; they work in the fields in summer and the forests in winter. With the mechanization of the 1950s, these two branches of the economy were able to free workers needed by other sectors. Nevertheless, rapid industrialization and urbanization have since taken a toll. Only 8.5% of the Finnish workforce now work in agriculture and forestry, down from 46% in 1950.

Although farms have increased in size, their numbers have declined and the area under cultivation has decreased. Most of the arable land is concentrated in southern Finland and consists mainly of vegetable gardens and fur farms. The most important crops are wheat, barley, oats, potatoes, rye, sugar beets, and oleiferous plants.

Dairy farming is the most important, making up two-thirds of the income from farming. Of the 450,000 dairy cattle and 300,000 head of reindeer in the country, most are found in Lapland. Finnish exports include eggs, meat, and dairy produce, of which the most famous is Finnish Emmenthal cheese.

WHERE MONEY GROWS ON TREES

Trees subjected to the ravages of acid rain.

Finland's most important natural resource is its forests, which cover about 70% of the country. Pine is the main species, accounting for about 40% of the annual growth rate, followed by spruce (37%), birch, aspen, and alder. Timber from the forests is used as roundwood in the sawmill, board, and plywood industries, or as fiber in the paper and pulp industries. The number of growing trees each year totals 58,622 million cubic feet (1,660 million cubic meters), while the annual felling rate is a little less than the annual increase of 2,472 million cubic feet (70 million cubic meters).

Finland's forests produce high-grade wood. Over 80% of all products in the wood industry are exported, accounting for 38% of the country's entire industrially processed output. Paper and pulp industries top the list. Finland is the second largest exporter of paper and cardboard after Canada.

Increasingly, the trees are being threatened with damage and destruction by acid rain, produced by a toxic combination of rain and air pollution originating in other countries. Large areas of trees have been affected.

Paper-lifting crane at United Paper Mills, one of about 30 paper factories in Finland.

PAPER PRODUCTION

Finland is one of the biggest suppliers of paper, accounting for as much as a quarter of the world's needs for printing and writing paper, ranking second after Canada. Yet paper is just one of the products of the all-important forest industry. This is not surprising as two-thirds of Finland is covered by forests, a natural resource that is renewed thanks to a conscious reforestation program. Apart from paper, the forest yields timber, plywood, pulp, paperboard, panel board, and other paper-related products.

The largest single exporter of paper to the world is Finnpap, which represents seven Finnish paper companies with 52 paper-making machines. In 1990, the total value of Finnpap's global sales was more than US$3.8 billion, which accounted for 74% of all of Finland's paper exports. It increased its production capacity from 1.4 million tons in 1960 to 8.5 million tons in 1991. The paper was sold to more than 100 countries, although the main markets are the United States, Great Britain, Germany, and France.

Apart from Finnpap, there are four other individual Finnish paper-producing companies. Their mills are big and modern, with fully integrated wood-processing units. Of all the paper products exported, one-sixth is newsprint, two-thirds is mechanical printing paper of mainly magazine paper grades, about 10% is woodfree paper grades, 5% is kraft paper, and the rest a wide variety of tissue, high-density, and other specialty papers.

INDUSTRY

Engineering and metal production are also important industries in Finland, making up nearly one-third of Finland's total output and also its exports. One out of every three industrial workers is engaged in these industries. Initially, industrial output went towards fulfilling Finland's war reparations to the Soviet Union. When these were fully repaid in 1952, the Soviet Union continued to be a market for Finnish metal and engineering products.

High-technology steel and copper production are the main sectors of the metal industry, while the mechanical engineering industry turns out machines and equipment for the agricultural, forestry, and wood industries; forklifts and trucks; electrical and electronic goods; and other consumer products. Other products are special seagoing vessels such as icebreakers, luxury ocean liners, and oil rigs adapted to extreme climatic conditions.

Finland is also well known for its advanced technology, such as the production of telephone exchanges, mobile telephones, cars, and electronic consumer goods such as television sets and handphones. The chemical industry has a 10% share of total industrial output. Apart from oil refining and fertilizers, the more important branches of the industry include techno-chemical and pharmaceutical production. There is also a demand for products such as textiles, clothing, leather, jewelry, decorative glass, furniture, and cutlery.

The energy industry in Finland is small. Only 30% of total consumption is

Cheese-filling press at an agricultural research center.

Local public trans-
portation in Helsinki
relies mainly on buses,
streetcars, and the
subway.

produced domestically, and the country relies heavily on energy imports from abroad. Traditional sources of domestic energy such as hydroelectric power, wood industry waste, and peat are now supplemented by nuclear power from four stations.

CONSTRUCTION

There was a construction boom in the 1960s and 1970s brought about by migration and urbanization as people moved from the countryside into towns. A huge housing program was drawn up and transportation networks such as roads, railways, canals, and harbors were extended. Nuclear power stations were built to provide more electricity. Industrial development also resulted in a mushrooming of new factories and offices.

In the 1970s the construction industry contributed 9% of the GDP, fueled by the building of some 70,000 housing units a year. The 1980s saw a slowdown in housing construction to about half the annual rate and building companies were forced to look abroad for contracts.

TRANSPORTATION AND COMMUNICATIONS

Finland's northerly geographical location, its small but widespread population, and its extremely varied climate have all been a mixed blessing. These have placed a burden on transportation and communications networks, but at the same time have helped to boost their development.

The country has a network of 46,000 miles (75,000 kilometers) of roads used by 2.2 million vehicles, 90% of which are privately owned cars. Road transportation is supplemented by railways; there are 3,700 miles (6,000 kilometers) of tracks. A quarter are electrified; the rest use diesel engines. Each major town has its own transportation network. In Helsinki, this includes suburban trains, buses, streetcars, and the subway.

In the 19th century, the Saimaa Canal was built to allow boats access to the lakes of eastern Finland. Other canals allow people, goods, and timber to be transported along lakes and rivers. Inland waterways, however, have been largely replaced by roads, although shipping is still important between the Baltic and Finnish lake districts.

The railway station in Helsinki, a city landmark, was designed by Eliel Saarinen and built between 1906 and 1914.

Finland has a well-developed domestic air network, recognized as one of the best in Europe. State-owned Finnair also has international links to major cities. The United States and Japan are among its long-haul destinations.

The Finns enjoy a superior telephone network and communications system. Automatic telecommunications cover the entire country and some 60 out of every 100 Finns own a phone, and 7% own mobile units.

FOREIGN TRADE

Because of the relatively small size of the domestic market, foreign trade is essential to Finland. The main exports in the first half of the 20th century were wood and paper products. In the 1950s, metal and engineering products took over as the chief exports because of huge orders from the Soviet Union. Finland's main trading partners are the European Free Trade Association (EFTA), which it joined in 1961, and the European Union (EU), which it joined in 1995. With its growing integration with Europe, Finland has diversified its major exports to include products from the metal, engineering, clothing, electronic, and chemical industries. The export share of traditional forest-related products has declined to 40%, down from 69% in 1960.

Nearly half of Finnish exports go to EU countries such as Germany, Britain, France, and Italy. Outside the EU, the biggest trading partner is Sweden, followed by the United States and Japan. Trade with Russia and countries making up the former Soviet Union fell after the latter's collapse, and now amounts to only 5% of total exports.

TOURISM

Finland receives two million foreign visitors each year. More than half of them come from the Nordic countries. The rest are mainly from other European countries, although an increasing number of tourists are arriving from as far away as the United States, Japan, and Southeast Asia. The tourist industry employs about 80,000 people and chalks up an annual turnover of over US$9.3 million. Revenue from tourism is about US$1.2 million, making it the country's fifth most important source of foreign income.

Although most visitors travel by air direct to Helsinki, many travel by ship or car ferry from Sweden, as Helsinki is an overnight journey from

Stockholm, the Swedish capital. Summer is the favorite season for travel in Finland, thanks to the warm weather and a full calendar of events, including several music and dance festivals. Lapland is a favorite tourist destination because it offers visitors a chance to experience the great outdoors, and they can pan for gold in many areas.

Flights by Finnair, the national airline, connect Helsinki and the rest of the country to major European cities, the American continents, and Asia, making Finland very accessible. Traveling in Finland is easy, as English is widely spoken.

Tourists looking at furs in a street market.

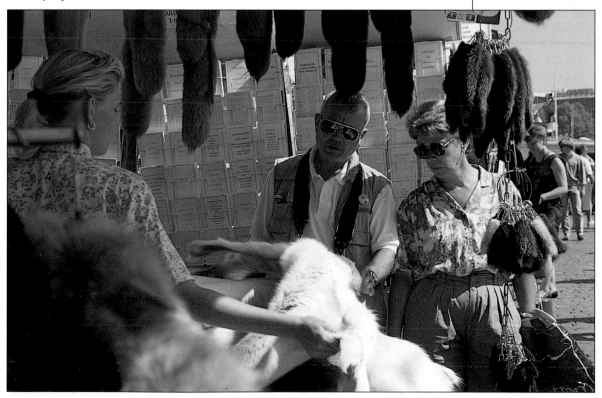

47

PEOPLE

AS A NORDIC PEOPLE, the Finns are generally expected to have blue or bluish-grey eyes, fair skin, and blond hair. Many Finns do fit this description, but there are also many dark-haired, brown-eyed Finns, a result of the continuing influx of people from the east throughout the area's long history.

Recent research into the hereditary nature of blood groups shows that about three-quarters of the present Finnish population are of western racial origin and the rest, eastern. The western element is strongest in the western part of the country and along the coast, the result of Scandinavian immigration in prehistoric as well as historic times. The eastern element comes from peoples migrating to Finland from the European part of Russia.

ORIGINS

The first people in Finland are thought to have been the tribes that moved into what is now Finland from the east after the Ice Age. At one time, most of Russia was inhabited by peoples speaking Finnish or languages related to it. These people were pushed west by invading Slavs. They were joined by Finno-Ugrian immigrants from the Baltic regions, who started settling about 2,000 years ago, first in Hungary and Estonia and later in Finland. These early Finnish speakers were followed by Germanic tribes who crossed the Baltic from the south and west.

Then the wave of Swedish settlers began when Sweden embarked on its colonization of Finland around the first millennium A.D., starting with the Åland Islands and moving into the coastal regions of the Gulf of Finland

Opposite and above: **For over 700 years, the Finns have resisted Swedish and Russian occupation and influences to retain their identity and fight for their independence.**

and the Gulf of Bothnia. Today Swedish Finns make up 6% of the population. They retain their own language and culture, but consider themselves to be citizens of Finland. Many others have blended into the ethnic mix that makes up Finnish people today.

The earliest Finns were presumed to have Mongoloid characteristics, and present-day Sami are believed to carry some of these genes. Today, the Finns consider themselves to be European but are proud of their heritage and language.

FINNS MAKE STEADFAST FRIENDS

"The common characteristics are: resilience, inner strength, patience, determination... a liking for the old and well-known, and a dislike for the new... steadfastness in duty, respect for the law, desire for liberty, honesty... a Finn is known for his reserve, for his caution. He needs time to relax and get to know people, but when he does, he is a trustworthy friend," wrote Z. Topelius in *Finland in the 19th Century*.

Says Finnish banker Kai Heinonen: "Finns are generally suspicious of outsiders because of centuries of isolation. They are also a shy people and until recently not many could speak English, so there was this language barrier with foreigners. But once you get to know a Finn, you will find he's trustworthy and will make a good friend."

Dogsleds are a time-honored method used by the Finnish people to move around in the wilds. The rides are popular with tourists as well.

POPULATION GROWTH

The first records of the size of the Finnish population appeared in the 1750s when there were said to be just under half a million people. This rose to over 800,000 by 1800. The growth rate was rapid in preindustrial times, as the numbers doubled to 1.769 million by 1870. It doubled again between 1870 and 1915 thanks to improved health conditions, medical care, and a drop in the death rate in the early stages of industrialization.

Since then, the birth rate has started to decline and the size of the population reached four million only after World War II and five million in 1992. During the 1980s, the government tried to increase the birth rate by encouraging families to have more children and offering incentives and benefits. The population is now growing at 0.3% annually, a very slow rate. The low birth rate, if it continues, is predicted to result in a fall in population in the future.

Children below the age of 5 make up almost 20% of the population.

POPULATION SPREAD

Finland is the third least populated country in Europe, after Iceland and Norway. Over half of all Finns (or 53.5%) live in three southwest provinces that make up only 15% of the land surface. The biggest town is Helsinki with nearly half a million people, followed by Espoo (176,000) and Tampere, which is the largest inland town with 173,803 people. About 75% of all Finns live in the urban areas.

The main towns have been in the south and southwest because of industrialization and the spread of commerce. After World War II, when Finland started to industrialize rapidly and people were freed from farming jobs because of mechanization, workers moved from the inland rural areas to where the factories and offices were in the southern region around Helsinki. In recent years, however, the migration of people from rural areas has stopped, so urban growth has slowed down.

The number of Finnish families emigrating in recent years has also had an influence on the population size. It is estimated that about a quarter million Finns (400,000 if dependants are included) have emigrated to Sweden. An even higher number—280,000—have left Finland to settle in the United States, while 20,000 have gone to Canada and 10,000 to Australia.

Finnish gypsies form the nation's largest minority ethnic group. Most of them live in the southern part of the country, where they continue to practice their age-old customs.

Finnish gypsies arrived in Finland during the 16th century when they were driven out of Sweden by the authorities.

THE SAMI

The tiny Sami minority in Finland live in the far north, beyond the Arctic Circle, in Lapland. There are estimated to be 2,000 pure-blooded Sami left, and they are the oldest inhabitants of the area. The Sami, sometimes called Lapps, were pushed northwards when the Finns arrived in present-day Finland from the east during the start of the Christian era. The Sami speak their own Sami language, which is part of the Finno-Ugric family.

The people live off the land much as their ancestors did and many are still nomads. They are experts at hunting and fishing and raise large herds of reindeer, upon which they depend for a living. The reindeer pull their sledges and transport their goods. The animals provide milk and meat, and their skins are used to make clothes and tents. The antlers of the reindeer are also highly prized and are carved into pieces of sculpture. The Sami sell souvenirs made from reindeer fur and bone carvings at roadside stalls along the northern highways.

The traditional dwelling of the Sami is a tent that is shaped like a Native American tepee. Called a *kota* ("KOH-ta"), it is a pole frame covered with reindeer skins. Inside, skins are also used to keep the ground warm, and in winter woven wool rugs keep the tent insulated.

The Sami have a colorful traditional costume in green, red, and blue. It is worn with an embroidered

A Sami man wears his people's distinctive native dress, rarely seen these days except on festive occasions.

Today, there are people of Sami descent who can be found living in Norway, Sweden, and the Kola Peninsula.

Traditional Sami dwelling. Many of the people now live in modern wooden houses.

cap. The upturned moccasin-like shoes that they wear in the winter are made from reindeer fur: so are gloves, leggings, and coats. Hay is placed inside the boots, and sometimes the gloves, for warmth.

Rovaniemi is the gateway to Lapland. It has a Sami village where the Sami way of life and customs are demonstrated to visitors. One custom is a typical Sami welcome that involves drinking reindeer milk from a small ceramic cup and having the milk poured down one's back!

THE FINNISH NATIONAL DRESS

The colorful Finnish national dress is based on the regional folk dress worn by Finnish peasants in the 18th and 19th centuries. Today it is worn mainly for family celebrations such as weddings and school or church events, or by those taking part in folk dances or performing in choirs.

The dress for men consists of a linen or cotton shirt, a vest, and a wool or cotton jacket teamed with a pair of trousers made from wool or chamois leather with knee breeches. Black leather shoes are worn with gray or black socks. A scarf wrapped around the collar and tied with a single knot, and a belt with key hook and knives complete the look.

The dress for women consists of a skirt and apron with a bow tied at the back. The top is a laced bodice. A scarf may be worn underneath the bodice or on top of it, tied into a triangle.

A headdress is usually worn. It can be a cap with a hard crown and lace, a white soft cap with lace, or an embroidered version of either one. A key hook hanging from the waistband and a pair of black shoes add the finishing touch.

There are craft schools that teach the making of the Finnish traditional dress.

A Finnish family in national dress, of which there are local and regional variations.

LIFESTYLE

FINNS, IN GENERAL, enjoy a high standard of living. As many of 60% of all Finns have a home of their own and 20% live in housing provided by the government. The remaining 20% live in rented homes. All this has been made possible by an enlightened housing policy adopted by the government in the 1950s to cope with the flow of rural folk to the urban areas. All housing areas are required to have basic amenities so residents are assured of a quality environment.

For the less well-off, the government gives low-interest and long-term loans of 15 to 20 years to help them buy homes of their own. Rents are kept affordable as they are controlled by the government and any increase is subject to state approval. In addition, families with children, elderly people, and students can apply for a housing allowance from the state to help them cope with the high cost of housing.

Opposite: **Winter temperatures and frozen lakes do not deter this fisher, who simply drills a hole in the ice and waits for the fish.**

Left: **The Finns love nature and the chance to retreat to holiday homes in the countryside. Nearly every lake, big or small, is dotted at the sides with tiny cabins where Finnish families spend their vacations.**

FAMILY STRUCTURE

Older Finns lament the influences of rapid modernization that are leading to the demise of some ancient customs and traditions. In the past, children would not leave home until they got married. Today, it is increasingly common for young university students to live on their own, and for couples to live together before marriage. But one family tradition is still strong—the Sunday lunch, when everyone in the family gathers in the home of the parents to spend time together.

The typical Finnish family spends about one-fifth of its combined household income on food. The home runs largely on electrical appliances. Cars, leisure, travel, cultural activities, education, hobbies, and electronic products absorb another 40% of the family income. As in many European countries, the traditional roles of men and women in the household have evolved into one of partnership. Family decisions and burdens are usually shared between husband and wife. Decisions like the kind of schools their children attend or where the family should live are made jointly.

A DAY IN THE LIFE OF A TYPICAL FINN FAMILY

Because hired help is expensive, few families can afford maids. It is the wife who usually does the household work with some help from the husband. She prepares the breakfast and sees the children off to school before she and her husband leave for the office or factory. No one goes home for lunch, which is eaten at school or the workplace. The family meets again for dinner at home. The evening meal is served early, at around 6 p.m. It is usually simple, because no one has time to prepare elaborate meals. The meal is also kept light because the Finns go to bed early.

The weekends are important days for the family because they can spend more time together. Much of it is spent on the great outdoors—going for walks, jogging, or birdwatching. During the summer, many families spend weekends at their lakeside summer house to fish, sail, or enjoy their sauna followed by a dip in the crystal-clear waters of the lake. In the fall, they go into the woods to pick berries and mushrooms or to admire the changing colors of the forest. During the winter, they go ice skating or skiing. The mother also has time over the weekend to cook more elaborate meals with soups, meats, and fresh fish.

In the evenings, with the children being looked after by a babysitter, the parents can take time off to go to the movies, the theater, or a concert.

Families like to spend time together enjoying nature on the weekend.

THE ROLE OF WOMEN

Women make up almost 50% of the workforce. Many serve in public office and head university departments and trade unions.

A young woman studies for her exams. In 1975 women accounted for 5.1% of physicists, 29.5% of doctors, and 98% of nurses. In 1981 Finnish women earned 61% as much as men.

Finnish women are proud of their privileged status. In 1906, they were the second in the world (after women in New Zealand) to be given the right to vote. Finnish women have equal chances with men to be educated right through university. They lead very independent lives, enjoy a status equal to men, and are allowed to keep their own name, if they wish to, after marriage. Many women have double names, adding their husband's name to their own. Most continue working even after they have families. It is estimated that women make up half of the student population in local universities, and about 70% of all Finnish women work outside the home.

As Finnish women themselves explain it, the reason for their independence stems from the important role they played in the days when the men were out hunting or fighting in wars and the women had to work on the farm and keep the household together.

The law allows married women paid leave for 258 days a year after the birth of a child. They are entitled to a further three years' unpaid leave from work, and their employer is obliged to keep their job open for them. Their husbands are also entitled to paid paternity leave of about two weeks.

Every woman is given a "mother's box," which is a maternity gift from the government, upon the delivery of a child. The box includes a mattress and can double as a bed for the baby. It comes with a toy and a gift pack of children's clothes, blanket, creams, hairbrush, and winter clothes. Cash is given if the mother prefers this, although the amount would be less than what is usually given in kind. All postnatal care is provided free.

Unlike past generations when the father was the undisputed head of the household, today's modern husband is likely to help his wife in most household chores and in bringing up the children.

MARRIAGE

Most Finns prefer to get married in church, whether or not they have been active churchgoers in the past. Couples usually choose to marry in spring or summer because of the favorable weather.

The man traditionally asks the father of his wife-to-be for her hand in marriage. There is no dowry, but a dinner celebration after the church wedding is hosted by the bride's parents at their home or in a restaurant. The Finns believe that whoever has his or her hand uppermost on the knife when the newlyweds cut the wedding cake will be the "boss" of the family. This also explains the custom of the bride and groom rushing to be the first to step on each other's foot!

After the cake-cutting, the dancing begins. The new couple has the first dance; the father of the bride then dances with her, while the groom dances with his new mother-in-law.

To mark the marriage, the parents of the bride also present gifts to the new couple. And on their first day as husband and wife, the groom

In 1981 a Finnish study showed that women and girls do twice as much housework as men and boys.

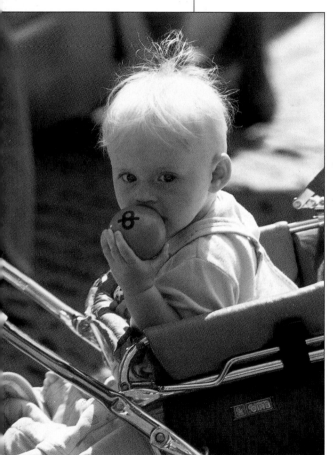

All children receive regular health checks under Finland's welfare system.

presents his wife with a gft of jewelry. In the past, the custom was for the groom to give a decorated wooden spindle so that his bride could weave clothes for the family. These days, if a spindle is given, it is used more as a decoration for the new home.

BIRTHS

The arrival of children is greeted with much fanfare in Finnish households. The father, who is often present during the delivery of the baby at a hospital, celebrates the occasion with his best pals the day after and gives out cigars to his colleagues at work.

When the mother and baby return home from the hospital, friends and relatives visit, bringing food, clothes, and other presents for the baby. A kind of pastry known as *rinkelli* ("RING-kel-li"), which is served with coffee, is also traditionally brought by visitors. One to three months later, a christening ceremony is held in the home. The baby usually wears a long dress made of lace, on which the names of those who have worn the same dress for christening are embroidered. This may include the baby's mother, father, or siblings.

The Finns traditionally leave their babies out on the open balconies of their homes to "get used to the fresh air," even during winter. They are warmly wrapped up, of course; it is believed that this makes them healthy.

Finland's infant mortality rate of six deaths in every 1,000 live births is one of the lowest in the world.

EDUCATION

Education is compulsory for children age 7 to 16. They attend comprehensive schools for nine years up to the ninth grade, then can choose to continue for another year into the 10th grade. Further education is voluntary. Students can attend upper secondary schools for three more years or enroll in a vocational school, where courses last from two to five years. These schools offer training in 25 trades and professions. Students can choose to qualify in the shortest period of time as a car mechanic, for instance, or specialize in a longer course that will qualify them as an engineer. Those taking the longer, specialized courses can enter the university. Finland has 17 universities and three art academies, with a total student enrollment of 80,000.

Free schooling is provided up to secondary level. For upper secondary education, students can apply for study grants or obtain low-interest loans. University students can turn to the state for state grants or to the banks for state-guaranteed loans. University students enjoy subsidies on health care, meals, and student housing.

During their early years of schooling, comprehensive schools equip children with a general education. At the upper secondary level academic subjects are studied unless the students are enrolled in a vocational school, where technical skills are taught instead.

A teacher minding her preschool charges at a daycare center.

PRESCHOOLS

Education for preschool children is voluntary. In practice, as more than three-quarters of mothers of preschool children are working, many of the youngsters end up in municipal daycare centers or in the private homes of approved babysitters where some form of teaching is given.

The Ministry of Social Affairs and Health and the local authorities work together to place young children of working parents into such daycare centers and homes. Although there is a shortage of such centers, the authorities plan to extend preschooling to all 5- and 6-year-old children. Currently, all children over 3 are guaranteed places if the need arises.

THE READING HABIT

Finland has one of the highest literacy rates in the world. Books are sold everywhere in Finland, ranging from popular magazines to novels, serious literature, and academic works. The Finns are avid readers who buy much of their reading material. They also make good use of an extensive network of free libraries, borrowing on the average 18 books and recordings per person a year. To support this habit, there are 1,500 public libraries and a big fleet of mobile libraries that serve 18,000 neighborhoods throughout the country. The libraries have over 30 million books, a million recordings, and an expanding video service. There are also about 600 scientific libraries offering 15 million books.

SOCIAL SECURITY

Finland has a well established form of social security backed by legislation. It is a welfare state that provides for the basic needs of all its citizens. Working Finns pay high taxes to fund the various programs under the system, such as health care benefits, protection for workers, and old-age pensions.

There are special family benefits as well, including paid maternity leave, child allowances, and free schooling, plus special programs that cater to the needs of the elderly and handicapped. The country's social security system is one of the best in the world, protecting Finns against all possible social risks.

HEALTH CARE

All residents in Finland are covered by a generous health care scheme. A nominal fee is charged for medical care, X-rays, laboratory fees, physiotherapy, and hospital treatment.

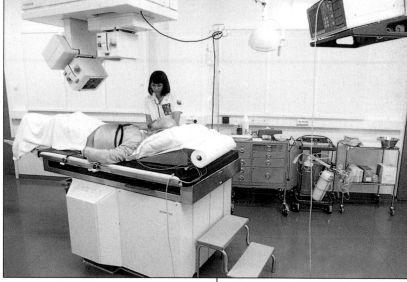

Most hospitals are government-run and the cost of treatment and medicine is heavily subsidized.

Expenses incurred from a hospital stay are refunded after a minimal deducation. Patients pay part of the cost of prescribed medicines.

Workers receive an allowance that works out to 80% of their salary for each day that they are ill, and for those who are not working, a minimum daily allowance is also given. Private medical care is also reimbursed after a certain amount. War veterans and those born in 1956 and after are entitled to free dental treatment.

A WELFARE STATE

Parents with children under the age of 17 are given child allowances. Those with children under 3 receive an additional allowance. Families with handicapped or very ill children under 16 are given home-care assistance.

Trade unions operate voluntary unemployment benefit funds upon which members can draw if they are laid off work. The funds are provided by the state, employers, and from contributions of the members themselves.

There is a maximum annual amount that can be paid as an unemployment allowance as well as over a three-year period. Workers not covered by union funds are paid an unemployment allowance by the state to meet basic needs.

Labor policy is regulated by law to protect both employers and employees. A standard employment contract covers working hours, annual vacation, and social benefits. Salaries and general wage increases are negotiated yearly.

In Finland, even those who have never worked receive a national pension once they reach the retirement age of 65. This applies to both men and women. In some occupations, the retirement age may be lower. The national pension is based on the wealth and income of each individual. For those who have worked before retiring, an employment pension linked to their previous earnings and number of years worked is also payable. The maximum employment pension is 60% of the last-drawn salary, but this is paid only after 40 years of work. If a person receives a large employment pension, his national pension will be smaller.

CARE OF THE AGED AND THE LAST DAYS

The elderly accounted for 13% of the total population of Finland in the early 1990s. Like other European countries, Finland's population is increasingly weighted toward the elderly.

The elderly in Finland prefer to be independent of their families, living in apartment blocks built specially for them so that they can get together with people of their own age. Municipalities also extend some help by arranging services such as cleaning, shopping, and cooking for a token fee. They also organize senior citizens' centers for the elderly to meet and obtain information. For those too old to look after themselves, there are senior citizens' homes.

When it comes to dying, the Finns prefer to have their elderly spend their last days in a hospital that can try to make their stay as comfortable and pain-free as possible.

As with marriage, the majority of Finns prefer to have a Christian burial even if they had never been active church members.

An old man in a hospital that specializes in the care of the elderly.

RELIGION

TODAY, 90% OF ALL FINNS belong to the Evangelical Lutheran Church, 3% to other denominations, and the rest profess no particular religion.

As a meeting point for two worlds, the East and West, Finland had to contend with the efforts of both sides to establish not just their political spheres of influence, but also their religious cultures: the Roman Catholic Church from the West and the Byzantine Orthodox Church from the East.

THE ROMAN CATHOLIC CHURCH

Christianity arrived in Finland by the end of 1000 A.D., but it was not until the middle of the 12th century that the Roman Catholic Church managed to gain a foothold in southwest Finland. This was largely the result of the first crusade waged by King Eric of Sweden and St. Henry, the bishop of

Opposite: **A traditional wooden church in Lapland.**

Left: **The medieval greystone church of Rauma near Turku in southwest Finland.**

A church on Turku Market Square shows the cruciform style.

Uppsala, to spread Swedish influence through missionary work.

The Roman Catholic Church used ritual, pomp, and pageantry in ceremonies to convert the nature-worshipping Finns who were familiar with rituals of their own. Masses were conducted mostly in Latin except for the Lord's Prayer, the Creed, and salutations to the Virgin Mary that were said in the local vernacular, Finnish. Incense, holy water, and other religious items were used for all ceremonies.

When Catholicism took root, the churches underwent a change. The first Finnish churches were built of logs. They were replaced by rough-hewn stone churches that were decorated with brick gables and shingle-covered, steeply pitched roofs. These churches soon became an integral part of the landscape in southwest Finland and the Åland Islands. In the 13th century, the country's only cathedral was built in Turku, which became the seat of the bishop.

In the 17th century, the basilica type of architecture was replaced by a style said to be more Protestant. Instead of a rectangular ground plan, a cruciform ground plan (shaped like a cross) was used, with the altar and pulpit situated near the intersection to allow the congregation a better view of church proceedings.

THE REFORMATION

The Reformation reached Finland in the 1520s. It was introduced in a gentle manner, in contrast to its Scandinavian neighbors, especially Norway, where reforms were pushed through regardless of opposition. The break with Rome took place in 1528 when Martinus Skytte was made the new bishop of Turku without first seeking the approval of the pope, as was required by canonical law.

The use of Latin in church services was replaced by Swedish, which was first used in 1531 in Turku Cathedral. By the end of the 1530s, bilingual services in Swedish and Finnish became the norm in churches. There was no opposition by the people in general to the changes brought about by the Reformation. Many did not understand the significance of the reforms, even though some did initially miss the ceremonial aspects associated with the Catholic liturgy.

The educational ties with southern Europe's old universities and cultural centers ended with the Reformation. Finns were now sent to study in places such as Wittenberg and Rostock in Germany, and Prague in what is now the Czech Republic. In 1642, a Bible in Finnish was finally produced.

SPEARHEADING THE MOVEMENT

In the 1500s, Finland lacked a university of its own so its best students were sent to further their studies in other parts of Europe. The Finnish scholar Mikael Agricola, for example, studied at the University of Wittenberg in Germany under Protestant reformer Martin Luther. He returned to Finland and introduced the revolutionary teachings of Luther and the Protestant Reformation to the Finns. The movement challenged the authority of the Roman Catholic Church.

The Lutheran Cathedral, with its distinctive dome and columns, stands in Helsinki's Senate Square. It was designed by C.L. Engel, who did not live to see it completed in 1852.

COUNTER REFORMATION

There was a brief resurgence of Catholicism coinciding with the reign of the Swedish King John III, in 1568. This Counter Reformation was the work of the Catholic Church in the newly Protestant countries of Europe. It all started when the Jesuits became dominant in the Stockholm Theological University. At the same time, John III favored bringing back some features of Catholicism, especially the ceremonial aspects. He came up with a blend of the two religious doctrines to be used in the Swedish empire, submitting it to the pope for approval. The plan was rejected, as some of his suggestions, such as allowing priests to marry, were controversial.

There was also opposition to John III's religious policy in Sweden and Finland, especially when he came up with the *Red Book* that outlined more Catholic forms of worship to be adopted in churches.

The Counter Reformation movement therefore did not gain a strong hold. The Protestant Church became firmly established in the latter part of the 16th and early 17th centuries. Legislation was passed prohibiting citizens from holding onto "sacramentalist, zwinglist, calvinist, anabaptist, or any other heretical doctrines." These were variant Catholic and Protestant movements. In 1617, the state went further by issuing a law that forbade conversion to Catholicism. Those who did so risked being banned from the country.

THE ORTHODOX CHURCH

The influence of the Orthodox Church was confined to certain areas in Finland where the dominance of Greek Orthodox culture had taken root since the Middle Ages. The appointment of Isak Rothovius as Bishop of Turku in 1626 gave the church a boost, as he was a supporter of Orthodox thinking.

The Orthodox Church was most dominant in the east, in Karelia, which looked towards Russia for spiritual guidance. For a time, during a movement to convert the Orthodox population to Lutheranism, many Orthodox followers crossed over the border to Russia to practice their faith. When Finland became an autonomous Grand Duchy of Russia from 1808 to 1917, the presence of the Orthodox Church became even more pronounced. There was an Orthodox church or chapel wherever a Russian garrison was stationed.

The Russian Orthodox Church flourished during the Russian occupation of Finland in the 18th century.

Today, the Orthodox Church continues to thrive. It is the second largest church in Finland with a membership of 60,000.

THE CHURCH'S ROLE

Finland is predominantly Lutheran today with about 600 parishes and more than 4.5 million followers, making it the world's third largest Lutheran congregation after the Netherlands and Germany. The 600 parishes are grouped under eight dioceses (districts under the jurisdiction of a bishop), each of which has its own bishop. Among the eight dioceses,

Women priests are a relatively new presence in Finland.

one is Swedish-speaking. All bishops are appointed by the Finnish president from a shortlist provided by each chapter. Turku continues to be the seat of the archbishop.

Although the country is basically secular because of the strong individualistic element in the largely Protestant society, the Church plays an important role in Finnish lives. More than 90% of all children are baptized and confirmed, and all Finns make it a point to attend church at some time or other in their lives. Whether or not they are active members, being married in church is considered obligatory, as well as being buried according to religious rites.

THE SYNOD

The Church Assembly, or Synod, is the highest decision-making religious authority. One-third of its members are drawn from the clergy and the rest from the lay public. The Synod looks after the operations of the churches and their finances. It also proposes changes to the Ecclesiastical Act, which must be approved by parliament.

The ordination of women priests—after a controversial debate—was consented to by the Synod in 1986. Parliament approved the amendment to the Ecclesiastical Act in 1988, the year when the first graduating class of women theological students was ordained. The office of bishop is also open to women.

FREEDOM OF RELIGION

As in many European countries, the church in Finland is no longer strongly bound to the state. Except for the right to levy taxes, the church is virtually independent. The church tax, paid by church members as well as companies, is collected on its behalf by the internal revenue department. The money pays for communal services provided the church, such as the keeping of birth and death registers and the maintenance of cemeteries.

Finland granted its citizens complete freedom of religion only in 1923. Depending on their beliefs, parents may have their children study religion at school or not.

The third most important church in Finland is the Pentecostal movement with a congregation of 50,000. The other churches are much smaller in membership and include Jehovah's Witnesses, Seventh-Day Adventists, the Finnish Free Church, and the Roman Catholic Church.

The Orthodox archbishop blesses the souls of the deceased in a ceremony held at a cemetery.

LANGUAGE

FINLAND IS BILINGUAL. Its two official languages are Finnish, spoken by 93.5% of the population as their mother tongue, and Swedish, spoken by 5.9%, or 300,000 people, who live mainly along the coast in the archipelago and around the Gulf of Bothnia. In Lapland, there are about 2,000 people who speak Sami, and in the south, about 5,500 gypsies have their own language.

With only about five million people in the world speaking Finnish and with very few foreigners knowing the language, which is difficult to learn, many Finns have learned to speak other languages—usually English, German, or some other European language.

Although it is part of Europe, Finnish has nothing in common with other European languages as it is not Indo-European in origin. Yet there are some borrowed words in Finnish—about 15%—taken from the Baltic,

Before the 19th century, Finnish poetry and folk tales reflected a strong Swedish influence. The Finns' pride in their own language and culture began to take root only in the latter half of the 19th century, thanks to the efforts of scholars like Mikael Agricola and J.V. Snellman.

Opposite and left: **Finnish as a language has its origins in eastern and northern Europe.**

A boy reads at a daycare center. Finland has one of the highest literacy rates in the world, and Finns are fond of reading. This is attributed to a tradition dating to the Church Law of 1686, which forbade marriage to anyone who couldn't read.

Slavic, Swedish, Russian, and Germanic languages, and several Finnish words are derived from French and English. Finnish is closely related to Estonian and, to some extent, Hungarian. Like these two, Finnish belongs to the Finno-Ugric group of languages, which is spoken by 23 million people worldwide. Sami is distantly related, but it is not easily understood by all Finns.

Unlike the English alphabet, the Finnish alphabet has three extra letters: Å, ä, and ö. Instead of five vowels, it has eight: a, e, i, o, u, y, ä, and ö. Finnish words tend to use many vowels and few consonants.

PRONUNCIATION

Finnish vowels are pronounced the same way as in English except for the following:

y is pronounced like the German *u*.

ä is like the *a* in *fact*.

ö is pronounced like the *e* in *theater*.

If a vowel occurs twice, as in *aa* or *ii*, there is a slight drag on the pronunciation, such as in *aah* or *ee*.

Certain consonants are pronounced differently from those in English:

z is pronounced as *ts* and can be written as such.

v and *w* are considered the same letter.

h has a weak sound except at the end of a closed syllable, when it is pronounced with more force, as in the German *ch* in *ich*.

j is pronounced like *y* in *yellow*.

r is rolled.

Double consonants such as *kk* in *Keskiviikka* ("KES-kee-VEEK-oh," or Wednesday) or aa in *saari* ("SAAH-ri," or island) are held longer. *Ng* and *nk* are two syllables and are pronounced as *ng-ng* and *ng-k*. For instance, *vangit* (prisons) is pronounced "VAHNG-ngit." The syllable *np* is pronounced as *mp*, so *olenpa* (I am) becomes "o-LEM-pa."

The Finnish language does not use articles of speech such as *a* or *the*. Prepositions are rare and the language does not distinguish between male and female pronouns—*he* and *she* are both referred to as *hän* ("hand"). As in French, Spanish, and other European languages, the Finns have two different ways of saying *you:* the informal *sinä* ("see-NA") when addressing close friends and relatives and the formal *te* ("tay") when speaking to acquaintances or at a professional level.

Teenagers talking. Most of the time, Finnish speakers place their emphasis on the first syllable of each word.

FORMS OF ADDRESS

Often, the Finns do not use forms of address such as Mr., Mrs., or Miss. Rather, they tend to address people according to their profession or status. For instance, a Mr. Rotko, who is the managing director of a bank, is called *Maisteri* ("MAIS-ter-ri") Rotko, meaning "bank director Rotko." A teacher will be addressed accordingly.

A STRANGE AND STUBBORN LANGUAGE

The Finnish language has been acknowledged as one of the most difficult to learn. Even though Finland is in Europe, its language is different from most of the other European languages. The languages closest to Finnish are Estonian and Hungarian, as these two, like Finnish, are Finno-Ugric languages. Although Finnish does not bear any relation to most European languages, its melodious intonations remind the visitor of Italian. A lot of vowels are used in Finnish; in fact, there are more vowels than consonants. Diphthongs (that is, *ai, ei, iu,* and *ou*) occur very often.

Consonants are so uncommon that Finnish words never begin with two consonants. For instance, the Germanic word *strand* ("SCH-t-ra-nd," meaning "shore") became *ranta* ("RUN-ta") in Finnish, with the two consonants dropped.

Words in Finnish can have many different forms—as many as 15 in some cases. Latin words only have six different forms. The form of a Finnish word depends on the context. For example, *talo* ("TA-lo") meas "house." To say "in the house," the word changes to *talossa* ("TA-lo-sa"), and to mean "of the house," it becomes *talon* ("TA-lon").

For a time, Finnish as a language was threatened when, during the periods of foreign occupation, languages such as Swedish and Russian

Finnish as a language tends to be long-winded. It is said that when translating, a 10-line text in English will end up as 12 lines in Finnish. Because the language is lengthy, goes a joke, a Finn has more time to think before he speaks, so that he does not end up speaking nonsense (like the speakers of other languages)!

were used instead. Despite much pressure, the patriotic Finns stuck to their own language. Like many other languages, however, new Finnish words have evolved over time to reflect outside influences, especially English. Thus, there is *rokkimusiikki* ("ROK-kee-MOO-see-kee") for rock music and *bandi* ("BARN-dee") for band. While some Finnish words are a bit of a tongue-twister, there are others you would be able to pronounce easily and even recognize their meanings right away:

hotelli ("HO-tel-li")	hotel
motelli ("MO-tel-li")	motel
auto ("AW-toh")	car
taksi ("TAK-si")	taxi
dieseli ("DEEY-sel-li")	diesel

To say "yes" in Finnish, it's *kyllä* ("KOO-la"), "no" is *ei* ("ay"), "thank you" is *kiitos* ("KEEH-tos"). For "please," you say *olkaa hyva* ("all-KAAH hoo-va") and for "goodbye," it is *nakemlin* ("NA-kem-een").

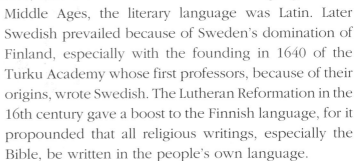

A statue of Mikael Agricola sculpted by Emil Wikstrom in 1908.

AGRICOLA—FATHER OF FINNISH LITERATURE

The man acknowledged to be the father of Finnish literature is Mikael Agricola (1510–1557), who created the Finnish written language. In the Middle Ages, the literary language was Latin. Later Swedish prevailed because of Sweden's domination of Finland, especially with the founding in 1640 of the Turku Academy whose first professors, because of their origins, wrote Swedish. The Lutheran Reformation in the 16th century gave a boost to the Finnish language, for it propounded that all religious writings, especially the Bible, be written in the people's own language.

It was Agricola who translated the New Testament in 1548 and the Psalms of David in 1551. He was among the first batch of students at the new University of Wittenberg to study under German Protestant reformers Martin Luther and Philipp Melanchthon, after the Reformation found its way to Europe. After three years, he returned to Finland, where he was appointed a schoolmaster in Turku, then a member of the cathedral chapter, before becoming a bishop in 1554.

His first work in the Finnish language was the Finnish ABC book, *ABCkirjai*, in 1543 followed by the Book of Prayer from the Bible that same year. The Finns are truly indebted to him, for it was Agricola who created the Finnish language, coining many new words that are still in use today. Thanks to his pioneering efforts, the complete Bible was finally translated in 1642, an enormous task that took nearly a century.

RADIO AND TELEVISION

Broadcasting in Finland began with ham radio operators in 1923. The *Suomen Yleisradio* ("SU-OH-men YU-lays-RA-dio," or Finnish Broadcasting Corporation), better known as YLE, was founded in 1926 to produce and air both Finnish-language and Swedish-language programs. Today, YLE broadcasts round the clock on three national stations and several local ones. Most Finnish households own at least one radio.

Watching television is also a favorite pastime, and most Finns spend about one to two hours a day in front of the television set. The most popular programs are locally produced films, serials, and entertainment programs.

Finnish households have at least one television set each, mostly in color, and many have video-recorder sets. They can tune in to several English-language channels and the French TV5 by means of cable networks.

The Finnish language has words borrowed from the Swedish, German, Baltic, and Slavic languages and, more recently, from English.

THE PRINTED PRESS

Finland's printed media has a history dating from 1771, when the first newspaper was published. The earliest magazines emerged at about the same time. It was only in the 1820s that Finland had more than one daily newspaper. They were in Swedish, as the readers were mainly Swedish-speaking. The oldest newspaper in Finland is the Swedish-language *Abo Underrattelser,* first published in 1824. The earliest Finnish newspapers date back to 1847.

THE ARTS

THE OLDEST FINNISH LITERATURE existed in the form of folk poetry, songs, proverbs, and legends, passed down from generation to generation by word of mouth. In other areas of artistic achievement, Fredrik Pacius penned the national anthem, *Our Land,* while Jean Sibelius composed orchestral music, with *Finlandia* as his best-known work.

RUNE SINGERS

It was not until the 16th century that folk poetry was first recorded. A 25-line commentary against the plague, written in 1564, is said to be the oldest manuscript of a folk poem recorded in the Finnish language. Previously stories were remembered through songs and ballads. It was the singers of runes, folk poems that are sung rather than read, who helped to ensure the survival of folk poetry. The skills of rune singing were often passed on in the family and a singer usually learned the lines from his or her parents. Tunes played on an ancient Finnish instrument, the harp-like *kantele* ("KAHN-tay-leh"), accompanied the poems.

Rune singers were primarily women, although the men tended to sing epic poems and women, the lyrical ones. In the 19th century, many of the rune singers were old and some were blind, like the well-known Miihkali Perttunen, the son of Finland's greatest rune singer, Arhippa Perttunen, who provided one-third of the material of *Old Kalevala.*

85

THE *KALEVALA* AND ELIAS LÖNNROT

The *Kalevala* is recognized as Finland's national epic. It is a compilation of ancient Finnish epic poems by Elias Lönnrot (1802–1884), recorded mainly from rune singers. The work took several years to finish and represented the first written collection of Finnish folk poetry.

Lönnrot was born to a poor family in a small village west of Helsinki. He learned to read at home and only started school when he was 12. He went on to study medicine and became a doctor, but his passion was in collecting Finnish folksongs. It was in the early 1830s that he had the idea of building up a series of minature epics based on the exploits of heroes such as Väinämöinen who were featured in folk poems. He later decided to combine them, publishing in 1833 the *Proto-Kalevala.*

In 1834, he was granted a scholarship by the Finnish Literature Society to travel and collect more folklore. The result was *Old Kalevala*, published in 1835. As time went on, the work grew bigger and bigger as Lönnrot gathered even more poetic material. All was this was compiled into the 50-canto *Kalevala,* which appeared in 1849 and has since been considered the foundation of Finnish culture. (A canto is a main division of a long poem.) It also stimulated interest in Finnish history and helped spark the movement for national independence. The epic has been translated into 43 languages and is the best-known work of Finnish literature worldwide.

Lönnrot collected much of his material in Karelia, where rune singers can still be found today. His work was a boost to the local arts. It sparked interest in the systematic collection of more folk poetry, now gathered in the Folklore Archive of the Finnish Literature Society, the biggest of its kind in the world. Folklore is accepted as a university field of study.

I have a good mind
take into my head
to start off singing
begin reciting
reeling off a tale of kin
and singing a tale of kind.
The words unfreeze
in my mouth
and the phrases are tumbling
upon my tongue they scramble
along my teeth they scatter.

— *A poem from the* Kalevala, *translated into English by Keith Bosley, 1989*

MODERN LITERATURE

A literary figure in the 19th century who was influential in shaping the Finnish national identity was Johan Ludvig Runeberg (1804–1877). The Swedish-speaking Runeberg lived in the rural backwoods of central Finland working as a tutor for a wealthy family on a country estate. He thus had opportunities to observe the life of the rural peasantry, romanticizing it in his first poems.

The Elk Hunters, written in 1832, rose to the status of a national epic. It was among the first works to be translated into Finnish by the newly launched Finnish Literature Society. But it was Runeberg's *Vanrinkki Stoolin Tarinat (The Tales of Ensign Stål)* that catapulted him to fame as a national poet. The ballad series was about Finland's war of 1808–1809 and the bravery of the Finnish soldiers fighting alongside Swedish troops. The first of these ballads was *Our Land,* which was later adopted as Finland's national anthem.

The works of J.L. Runeberg were written in Swedish and translated into Finnish.

Half of Finland's writers and poets are women.

Aleksis Kivi (1834–1872) wrote the first novel in Finnish, entitled *Seven Brothers.* The stubbornness, endurance, and love of liberty of the brothers of the story continue to elicit the admiration of Finns today. Minna Canth (1844–1897) was the first major Finnish playwright. Her works, drawing on her experience as a wife and widow, were an inspiration to the workers' and women's movements. The best known novel in Finland is *The Unknown Soldier* by Väinö Linna. A powerful antiwar statement, it is a realistic portrayal of war from the point of view of an ordinary soldier.

Below: **Folk musicians in Helsinki, and Jean Sibelius with two of his daughters.**

Opposite: **Dancers perform a modern ballet.**

MUSIC

For many years, traditional folk music dominated the Finnish scene. It was not until the 19th century that composers moved away from its melodic tunes to draw inspiration from other sources. Since then, many performers and composers have established a reputation for themselves abroad.

The first notable name in Finnish music was Fredrik Pacius, who composed the score for *Our Land*. He also set up the first orchestra and choir in Helsinki.

Finnish opera singers have also met with success on the international stage. Soprano Aino Ackté set the pace in the early 1900s. She founded the Savonlinna Opera Festival, which helped to nurture future opera talents. Finnish pianists, cellists, and conductors have also acquired international fame and lately, jazz musicians as well.

The Finns are also fond of light music by dance bands and, for many years, Toivo Kärki reigned as the most popular composer and Dallapé, the best dance band.

JEAN SIBELIUS

Jean Sibelius is Finland's best known composer. His name has become equated with Finnish music throughout the world. His *Finlandia,* for which he drew inspiration from the local landscape, became an anthem of the Finnish independence movement. For many years the Russians refused to allow it be performed because it expressed so much national pride.

However, Sibelius is also part of a greater European musical tradition. He had traveled to Munich and Bayreuth in Germany in 1894 and was influenced by Tchaikovsky and German symphonic composers like Wagner and Beethoven. His *First Symphony,* first performed in 1899, signalled a step in moving away from his national heritage. In his later compositions, particularly the *Sixth Symphony* (1923) and *Seventh Symphony* (1924), Sibelius came into his own as a composer, unbridled by time or place. The 1920s marked his international recognition as a composer. His symphonies, as well as *Finlandia* and a composition called the *Karelia Suite* (1893), are played by orchestras all over the world. His works have created an awareness of Finland among people in the rest of the world.

DANCE

Folk dances are still very much a part of the cultural landscape, but these days they are performed mainly at special events and outdoor festivals. The modern dance movement, on the other hand, is gaining popularity. It only began in 1922 when the Finnish National Ballet was set up as part of the Finnish National Opera, which was founded in 1911. The company presented *Swan Lake* in

A folk dance performed in traditional costume.

the Russian classical ballet tradition on its opening night.

While Margaretha von Bahr is considered the doyenne of Finnish dancers, it is Jorma Uotinen who is credited with revolutionizing Finnish dance. Uotinen, who had switched from the National Ballet to modern ballet, is Finland's best known choreographer outside the country.

The yearly Kuopio Dance and Music Festival—the only one in Scandinavia—has helped to enhance the reputation of Finnish dance theater.

CINEMA

The film industry is relatively new. It started in 1906, and the first talking movie was made in 1931. Television has been the cinema's greatest competitor; as a result, only an average of 15 feature films are produced each year. Still, some Finnish directors such as Jorn Donner and Rauni Mollberg have received international acclaim. The best-known Finnish film is Edvin Laine's *Tuntematon Sotilas* (*The Unknown Soldier),* adapted from Väinö Linna's novel.

THEATER

Theater in Finland began with the practice of ancient folk rituals associated with hunting and fishing. These pagan customs died out with the arrival of Christianity, which then developed its own theatrical arts.

Although the earliest drama performance in Finland was held in Turku in the 1650s, it was not until the 19th century that the first theaters were built. The first Finnish play, *Silmänkääntäjät* (*The Conjurers*) by Pietari Hannikainen, was performed in 1847, but the 1869 presentation of Aleksis Kivi's *Lea* was said to be the year when Finnish-language theater really took off. Finland has more than 40 professional theatrical groups and as many amateur and youth groups.

Theater performance in Savonlinna, where an opera festival is held every summer at Olavinlinna Castle.

ARCHITECTURE

Some of the older buildings in Finland reflect the country's early Swedish and Russian influences. The Finnish style only found expression from the 18th century and can be seen in its medieval stone castles, churches, and the detailed carvings of its 18th-century wooden churches and bell towers. Carl Ludvig Engel (1778–1840), who designed the neoclassical center of Helsinki, is the best known name in 19th-century Finnish architecture.

The Romantic architectural style at the beginning of the 20th century was a blend of Karelian wooden architecture, medieval stone work, and Art Nouveau style. The 1920s saw the development of the more severe lines of classical architecture, followed by more functional designs as characterized by the works of Alvar Aalto (1898–1976), the father of modern Finnish architecture. Aalto has been influential in regional and urban planning, the design of homes, churches, and larger buildings, as well as interior decoration and industrial art. His last important work was Finlandia House in Helsinki, a monumental meeting center in white marble. He considered the forest to be Finland's most important resource and continually created links back to the forest. Aalto's wife, Aino Marsio Aalto (1898–1949), is seen today as an important contributor to Aalto's work. She provided the social conscience and followed through after Aalto made the initial sketches.

A particularly well known Finnish architect is Eliel Saarinen (1873–1950), who designed the Chicago Tribune Building, which set the standard for early skyscrapers in the United States. His son, Eero Saarinen (1909–1961) is known for his design of the TWA terminal at Kennedy Airport in New York City. The terminal looks like a giant prehistoric bird poised to take off in flight.

Raili Pietilä (1923–) works with her husband, Raimo Pietilä (1923–), on many projects, including churches, town centers, and the presidential residence. They have been described as unconventional, searching for new ideas.

A high point of Finnish architecture can be seen in the new town of Tapiola. Created in the late 1950s, Tapiola brought together the talents of the most important Finnish architects and urbanists of the time, including Alvar Aalto, Aarne Ervi, Pauli Blomstedt, and Raili and Raimo Pietilä.

Today the emphasis of Finnish architecture lies in creating a more human touch and harmony with the environment. The restoration and conservation of old buildings is an area of particular interest.

"This nation faces any storm like mountain rock. Its joy is in tranquility, but in its travail it would be content to eat of hunger's bread while spurning alien grain."

—*Finnish poet Eino Leino*

Mother of Lemminkainen by the River of Tuonela, a 1862 oil painting by Robert Wilhelm Ekman based on the *Kalevala.*

PAINTING AND SCULPTURE

The earliest examples of art in Finland are the Stone Age carvings on rocks left by Arctic hunters and the frescoes in the country's medieval stone churches.

Finnish art as we know it really began with the founding of the Fine Arts Society of Finland in 1848. The greatest strides were made in the 1890s, when interest in the *Kalevala* and Finnish folk poetry was revived, and many artists turned to nature and Karelia as the origin of their cultural past. This gave rise to a movement known as Karelianism that had themes centered around landscapes and fauna. It led to the flourishing of a period that was acknowledged as the golden age of Finnish art—around the end of the 19th century. The famous names of this era included history painter Albert Edelfelt, Akseli Gallen-Kallela, Eero Järnefelt, Pekka Halonen, and Juha Rissanen.

In sculpture, Waino Aaltonen's portrayal of Paavo Nurmi, the Olympic runner, is internationally known. Eila Hiltunen created the first completely abstract monument to a person in the Sibelius Monument in Helsinki, which recalls the shape of organ pipes. In response to criticism, Ms. Hiltunen added a representation of the composer's face.

Finnish design tran-
scends cultural barriers.

DESIGN

The Finns are masters of design, gathering their inspiration from nature. The curving shores of Finnish lakes, for instance, are said to have influenced the works of many artists, such as Alvar Aalto's celebrated Savoy vase.

Finnish textiles and rugs reflect the colors of changing seasons, while glass designers adopt many motifs from flora and fauna. Wood remains the most popular material for designers working by hand.

Finnish design was taught as early as the 19th century and made its international launch at the Paris World Exhibition in 1900. It has a classic quality about it. Its clean, modern lines have an element of timelessness. The designs are also practical, as reflected in Marimekko's popular textiles for household use, the enamel kitchenware of Heikki Orvola, and the household articles of Timo Sarpaneva. Tapio Wirkkala, a glass designer known for his iceberg designs, Kaj Franck, known for his textures, ceramics, and glass, and Timo Sarpaneva, known for his graphic design, ceramics, and glass, have acquired international reputations.

The artistic designs found in glass and silver objects are akin to sculpture and are good buys for tourists hunting for typical Finnish products to take home as souvenirs. Equally avant-garde in design are jewelry and furniture. Many Finnish designers also create designs for industry, and the lines between art and design are constantly blurred.

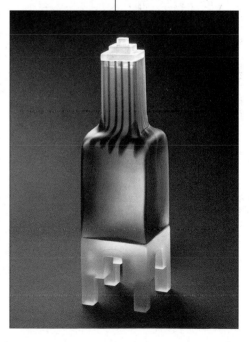

LEISURE

THE FINNS ARE A PEOPLE who love the outdoors, which is not surprising considering how much open space they have. For hundreds of years, they have been subjecting themselves to tests of strength, endurance, and speed. They have built up over the years, for instance, a strong reputation as long-distance runners performing well in marathons.

From as early as 1640, the Royal Academy of Turku had a swordsmanship instructor. Sports were incorporated into military life back in the 1780s and the army has, to this day, relied on long-distance cross-country skiing as a means of developing the endurance of conscripts.

Even preschool children start out in sports early in life and often continue when they are senior citizens. Winter sports, especially cross-country skiing, are popular. Mass skiing events each weekend during the winter season help to fuel enthusiasm for the sport. The biggest annual

Opposite: **Fishing is a favorite leisure activity for Finns.**

Left: **People playing chess in Hesperian Park in Helsinki.**

The Finnish countryside beckons hikers with its lakes, hills, and wooded terrain.

event is the 47-mile (75-kilometer) Finlandia Skiing Marathon from Hämeenlinna to Lahti, which attracts well over 10,000 participants. When the snow season is over, the traveler can often spot Finns out on the road, looking as if they were skating on shortened skis. They are actually training for long-distance skiing using special mini-skis fitted with wheels.

Swimming also has a strong mass following and thanks to heated indoor pools, the sport can be practiced even in winter. Other popular sports are orienteering, cycling, jogging, soccer, and *pesäpallo* ("pay-SA-PARL-lo"), a sort of baseball. Although soccer is popular, the Finns are nowhere near the top of the European league. American football is also played and the Finns have become European champions in the game. There are also ample opportunities for fishing and boating, as so much of the country is covered by water.

The sports that draw the largest number of spectators are soccer, ice hockey, track-and-field events, and skiing. There is probably a club for every kind of sport in Finland, with several clubs spread out through the country for the more popular sports.

HIKING

Finland's vast areas of wilderness make it a wonderful place for hiking. In the fall Finns often go for walks in the forest to gather mushrooms and pick wild berries. A network of well-marked trails and closely spaced footpaths make hiking easy even for someone unfamiliar with the Finnish forest. The Finns have a choice of 29 nature reserves in which to do their hiking. These have wilderness huts and camping facilities for overnight hikers.

Finland's thousands of lakes offer many opportunities for fishing. The best time for fishing is in spring and fall.

WATER SPORTS AND FISHING

With a total coastline of 25,000 miles (40,000 kilometers), which includes the mainland and thousands of islands, boating is big business in Finland. In summer, canoeists take to the lakes, rivers, and even the seas around the skerries and islets of the Åland archipelago. Out in the open sea and along the coastline, the sails of yachts and dinghies dot the horizon. The waters around the Åland Islands are also popular sailing grounds. The boating season is from late May to late September.

The Finns enjoy angling for fish when they are on a picnic by a stream or lake, and pan-frying their fresh catch out in the open air. Anglers can also fish from boats out at sea or from the coastline. The species of fish usually caught are perch, cod, pike, whitefish, rainbow trout, sea trout, and Altantic salmon. Even in winter, when the lakes usually freeze, the Finns still fish simply by making a hole in the ice!

Men enjoy elk hunting for its team spirit and cama-raderie.

HUNTING

Hunting is another favorite pastime, particularly for elk, hare, deer, and birds like black grouse and capercaillie. Each year, as many as 40,000 licenses for hunting elk are issued. Permits are also required from landowners, and these are usually handled by hunting associations, of which there are 3,500 in Finland.

The hunting season starts at the end of August with all the ritual it involves. The participants are usually men, for whom it is a form of camaraderie as they share the tasks of camping, picnicking, and stalking prey in the woods or out on lakes in boats, or with a dog if they are hunting birds.

HARNESS RACING

An unusual sport is harness racing, a spin-off from horse-riding, which is also popular. Also called trotting, harness racing is a big spectator sport. About 700 races are held annually. The biggest track in Finland is Vermo, just outside Helsinki, which ranks among the largest in Europe. About 80 races a year are held there, usually on Wednesdays and Sundays.

SHOOTING RAPIDS

Shooting rapids on large rubber rafts is a popular pastime enjoyed by young and old on a number of rivers. Operators of this activity provide the necessary equipment of life jacket, waterproof trousers, and rubber boots.

THE OLYMPICS

Finland's first entry into the Olympics was in 1906 at the intermediate games held in Athens. It marked its participation with a victory in wrestling by Verner Weckman. The country was then part of the Grand Duchy of Russia.

In 1912, Finland won nine gold medals at the Stockholm Olympics. Three were won by long-distance runner Hannes Kolehmainen, who snatched victory in the 5,000-meter and 10,000-meter events, and in the marathon. From 1906 to 1988, Finland has won 133 Olympic gold medals, of which 32 were in the Winter Games.

The Finns are especially strong in long-distance running and javelin events. Two runners in particular have made a name for themselves in sports: Paavo Nurmi and Ville Ritola. The famous Paavo, said to have "run Finland onto the map of the world," was the most famous Finnish athlete of all time. He won nine gold and three silver medals in the Olympics between 1920 and 1928. Ville won five golds.

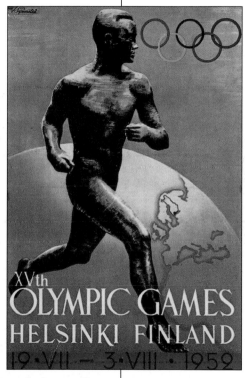

A poster publicizes the Olympic Games held in Helsinki in 1952.

In more recent times, the top name in running is Lasse Virén. He won the 5,000-meter and 10,000-meter events in the 1972 and 1976 Olympics.

In javelin, Finland has swept triple victories three times, and in the 1988 Seoul Olympics, the Finns won the gold and bronze medals. In the 1992 Barcelona Olympics, Finland walked away with a silver.

Finland dominated wrestling events in the Olympics in the 1920s. Although track-and-field has ruled since then, the Finns have also made a mark in other sports such as gymnastics and even canoeing. Top oarsman

Finnish cross-country skier Marja-Liisa Kirvesniemi brought glory to her country by winning four Olympic medals in 1984.

Perti Karpinnen, who was Finland's sportsman of the year in 1979 and 1980, and Mikko Kolehmainen, who won a gold in the 1992 Barcelona Games for canoeing, have boosted the popularity of these sports.

The Finns are also top contenders in winter sports, winning numerous gold medals in cross-country skiing in the Olympic winter games and world championships. Ski champions in the past have been Veli Saarinen, Veikko Hakulinen, and Eero Mäntyranta among the men, and Helena Takalo and Hikka Riihivuori for the women.

Marja-Liisa Kirvesniemi was the darling of the nation when she snatched three gold medals and one bronze for cross-country skiing in the 1984 Sarajevo Winter Olympics. Her husband, Harri Kirvesniemi, is also a champion skier in his own right, having won medals in the Olympics and world championships. The latest skiing star is Marjo Matikainen, who won a gold and two bronze medals in the 1988 Calgary Winter Olympics.

The Finns are equally strong in ski-jumping. The most famous Finnish ski-jumper is world master and Olympic champion Matti Nykänen, who was unsurpassed in this event in the 1980s. In the Calgary Winter Olympics, he became the first ski-jumper ever to win three golds in the same games. A ski-jump is named for him in his hometown of Jyväskylä.

Toni Nieminen made a name for himself when he became the youngest winner ever in the history of the Winter Olympics. He won two gold medals and one bronze for skiing in the 1992 Olympics in Albertville, Canada. He also won a gold medal in the 1992 World Cup.

Ice hockey is just as popular, with junior leagues formed for promising youngsters. Some Finnish players like Jarri Kurri have done so well that they have moved to the United States to join professional teams, as it is not possible to be a professional hockey player in Finland.

MOTOR SPORTS

The Finns also shine in motor racing. Well-known names who have won many world events include Markku Alen, Ari Vatanen, Timo Salenen, Juha Kankkunen, and Hannu Mikkola.

Pekka Vehkonen dominates in motorcross racing, while Keke Rosberg achieved a first when he became Finland's first Formula One driver, winning the world championship in 1982.

SUPPORT FOR SPORTS

Finland has several sports associations that are umbrella bodies for clubs and their members. The biggest association is *Suomen Valtakunnan Urheiluliitto* ("SU-OH-men VARL-ta-KOO-narn OOR-hey-loo-LEE-to," or the Finnish Central Sports Federation). The associations usually award training grants to top athletes who are their members. Olympic participants are given funds by the Finnish Olympic Committee.

There are specialized sports institutes in the country and centers of research and instruction. The major centers are the University of Jyväskylä, the University of Tampere, and the UKK Institute (named for President Urho Kekkonen), also in Tampere. Funding for sports comes from the

"We Finns have never been brilliant team players. But we shine in those sports that demand courage and the ability to make independent decisions. That's how Lasse Virén, Paavo Nurmi, and many others have succeeded in grueling long-distance running. That's also the way that we struggle by ourselves in rallies against the clock. Finns don't want to lose!"

—Rally driver Markku Alen

state-owned *Oy Veikkaus Ab* ("OR-oo VAYK-hows AH-BAY"), which operates football pools, trotting races, the national lottery, and other smaller lotteries.

Winners in international competitions are usually given a hero's welcome and even rewards such as houses financed by generous donors. Finland's interest in sports is demonstrated by the number of world sporting events it has hosted. These included the 1952 Olympic Games, which signalled the country's acceptance into the international fold, and the first World Athletics Championships in 1983, both of which were held in Helsinki, and several world ice hockey and skiing championships.

A statue of long-distance runner Paavo Nurmi, "the Flying Finn," stands outside the Olympic Stadium in Helsinki.

THE FINNISH SAUNA

If there is one single item that is quintessentially Finnish, it it the sauna. The sauna was traditionally used as a kind of bath-house. When people lived in forests, they had a log cabin where they could keep a fire going to keep warm, relax, and wash themselves. Babies were also born in the sauna, as it was the only warm place then. And when houses had no shower or bathrooms, a weekly visit to the sauna was the only way to keep clean.

Today, the sauna has endured. Even though modern homes are equipped with modern bathrooms, it is still a tradition for families and friends to get together in the sauna to relax. It has become a social ritual.

Many homes have private saunas; for those that do not, there is a sauna in every apartment complex. Families with second homes by the lake and those living in rural areas have a separate log cabin housing the sauna, where they gather on Saturday evenings to relax.

The sauna tradition is well-suited to Finland's forests, which supply building materials and fuel. The traditional smoke sauna, which has no chimney, is preferred, as the heat is said to be more gentle. It takes seven hours to bring the sauna to the right temperature, and all smoke is expelled before anyone goes in. It is a tradition to jump into the lake to cool off between visits to the sauna, or to roll in the snow if it is winter.

The Finns also use birch leaves to clean themselves in their sauna—it has the same effect as soap—and they hit each other with *vihta* ("VEE-ta") twigs to stimulate blood circulation and "beat out" tiredness from the body. After the cleansing ritual, the Finns indulge in a "sauna supper." Any Finn who invites a guest to take a sauna prepares a meal or at least coffee. While in the sauna, much salt is lost from the body due to perspiration, so salted dishes are usually served during the meal. These may include salted herring eaten with hot boiled potatoes, anchovies, smoked fish, sardines, or a salad of salted mushrooms.

FESTIVALS

FINNISH FESTIVALS HAVE PAGAN roots and in ancient times, when farming was the main activity, were linked to the seasons. The traditional relationship of the Finns to nature can be traced to the time when they worshipped the many gods and spirits that symbolized nature and the elements. The most important god of all was *Ukko* ("OO-ko"), the god of thunder and lightning, and his wife *Rauni* ("RA-ow-nay"), mother nature, both of whom were believed to take care of the weather and seasons. *Ukko* gave the Finns their word for thunder: *ukkonen* ("OO-ko-nen").

Christianity came to Finland at the end of 1000 A.D. but could not wipe out the old beliefs that were part of everyday life. In fact, the Finns simply transposed ancient rituals linked to nature into celebrations of Christian feasts and saints. Even after the Reformation in the 1520s when Catholicism and the old saints were dropped in Finland, the old legends and traditions survived.

EASTER

Although Easter is a church festival and Christian in origin, in Finland it is linked to ancient customs such as the burning of bonfires to prevent witches and spirits from harming precious farm cattle.

An early Catholic tradition was burning a scarecrow-like effigy of Judas in the bonfire on Good Friday. These days, however, customs have changed. Young girls, disguised as witches, are armed with willow twigs decorated with colored paper and feathers. They go from house to house to wish people good luck and prosperity.

Opposite: **Celebration of the Festival of Light, or Lucia Day, on December 13. The festival is Swedish in origin and reflects the Swedish influence on Finland's history and culture.**

Below: **Easter decorations include chicks, eggs, pussy willow, and a straw doll. In Finland, the occasion is a curious blend of religious and pagan practices.**

Folk traditions and customs from Sweden, Russia, and Germany exist alongside Christian beliefs to create the many holidays and celebrations observed in a year.

SHROVE TUESDAY

Laskiainen ("LAS-kee-ah-nen"), or Shrove Tuesday, is celebrated seven weeks before Easter. It used to be a time for merrymaking as it signalled the end of the annual work cycle and was just before the beginning of Lent when people were expected to be austere in their behavior.

SLEEPYHEAD DAY

According to Finnish custom, anyone sleeping late on this day will feel tired for the rest of the year. The Finns call the day *Unikeonpäivä* ("OO-nee-KAY-on-pai-va") and it falls on July 27. It commemorates the ancient legend of the seven martyrs of Ephesus who fled from the tyrannical Roman Emperor Decius in A.D. 249, spending the years until A.D. 447 sleeping in a cave. Sleepyhead Day is still celebrated in places like Naantali and Hanko.

CHRISTMAS

The greatest rejoicing is at Christmas, the most important event of the Finnish festive calendar year. It coincides with the darkest day of the year (December 23), which was celebrated long before Christianity came to Finland. Known as *Joulu* ("YO-lo"), it symbolized, in ancient times, the end of the harvest and thus was an occasion for feasting. Also, it marked the beginning of winter when food was collected and stored to last the long, cold season. There was reason to rejoice before the hardship began.

The Christmas tree was only introduced in the last century but has now become an integral part of the Finnish Christmas. Originally, Father Christmas appeared in the form of a goat, throwing presents into the doorways of houses. The appearance of a goat stems from the pagan days when the

worship of Thor, the Swedish god of thunder, included his goat. In the past, someone would masquerade as a goat and carry a goat's head, bursting onto parties of merrymakers. After nightlong celebrations of singing and dancing the goat would "die" and then return to life.

In 1927, a children's radio program introduced the modern Father Christmas with his home in Lapland, bringing gifts to children in his reindeer-drawn sleigh. The notion has stuck. Today, children the world over are enticed to spend winter holidays in Lapland with a resident Santa Claus. His "home" is decked with all kinds of Christmas-related items and he answers letters sent by those unable to visit him in person.

Santa Claus has a workshop in Lapland near Rovaniemi, and there is a special post office that replies to cards and letters received from all over the world.

BOXING DAY OR SAINT STEPHEN'S DAY

Known as *Tapaninpäivä* ("TAH-pa-neen-PAI-va"), December 26 was a day when people would ride in sledges drawn by foals harnessed for the first time, an event to commemorate St. Stephen, the patron saint of horses.

Midsummer bonfires lend an air of festivity. In Finland, weddings at Midsummer are quite popular.

THE MIDSUMMER BONFIRE

Midsummer is a festival of light, celebrating the summer solstice, when the day is at its longest. The celebration usually takes place on Midsummer Eve, or the eve of the Feast of St. John the Baptist on June 23.

Known as *Juhannus* ("yu-HAHN-os") in Finland, the celebration is said to be early Christian in origin. It was believed that the doors of the underworld were open on this day, letting out spirits and ghosts to roam the streets and infest the air. Thousands of bonfires are lit in the belief that, by burning a bonfire, the air will be purified so that the spirits can do no harm.

Others believe that the event is most likely a folk tradition associated with this magical nightless day. That it was the day of the most light was reason enough for merrymaking. It was also a celebration associated with growth, life, and fertility.

Cattle were decorated with garlands of flowers, while young maidens would sleep with a sprig of nine herbs under their pillows so that they would dream of their future bridegrooms. If girls looked into a pool of water, it was said that they could see the face of their sweetheart. Many of these customs are still practiced today as a source of amusement.

Other customs date back to pre-Christian times, when magic was used to promote a bountiful harvest and fertility in the coming year. Houses, boats, and buses are covered with fresh birch branches. In many places in Finland, doorways continue to be adorned with young birch trees, while those living on the Swedish-speaking Åland Islands put up Midsummer poles. These poles, erected in the midst of a bonfire pile, are decorated with wooden ships and boats and people dance around them. Midsummer supper tables are decorated with birch and flowers.

Midsummer bonfires are lit throughout Finland. Families and friends gather at lakeside cottages to make their own bonfires, dancing around them and singing traditional songs. They stay up all night celebrating. The biggest bonfire in Helsinki is at the Seurasaari open-air folk museum, where cultural dances are also held as part of the festivities.

NAME DAY

The Finns celebrate two birthdays a year! One is the day when they were born and the other is the day of their name. The Finnish calendar is filled with days that have one or more names and the day bearing your name is considered your Name Day. The tradition evolved from saints' days observed in the past by the Roman Catholic Church.

It is customary for friends and relatives to wish the Name Day boy or girl a "Happy Name Day" and to give flowers and presents. It is also celebrated with a birthday cake and candles.

Ruut (Ruth) Rotko, who celebrates her name day on January 4 and her birthday on May 27, says: "People always know your Name Day but not necessarily your birthday."

"Widespread they stand, the Northland's dusky forests, ancient, mysterious, brooding savage dreams; Within them dwells the Forest's mighty god, and wood-sprites in the gloom weave magic secrets."

—*Finnish composer Jean Sibelius*

A Midsummer pole stands in the Åland Islands.

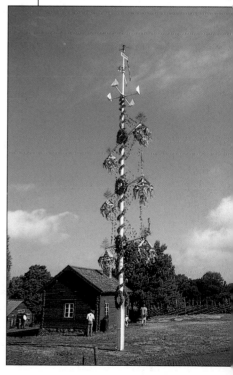

111

INDEPENDENCE DAY

Finland's Independence Day, on December 6, is one of the country's most important dates. If the weather pattern is normal, there is likely to be a fresh blanket of snow to enhance the day's celebrations. Different parts of the country have their own festivities to commemorate the day in 1918 when Finland became an independent republic.

Helsinki, as the nation's capital, is the most important place for celebrations. These start at 9:00 in the morning with a flag-raising ceremony. A commemorative daytime service is then held.

In the afternoon, there is a procession from the Hietaniemi Graveyard to Senate Square. This solemn procession of university students is perhaps the most moving of all the commemorative ceremonies. The event is held to remember those who died in helping Finland gain its independence. Lighted candles are placed on the graves to burn all evening, illuminating the dark, snowy stillness—a befitting end to the day's events.

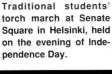

Traditional students' torch march at Senate Square in Helsinki, held on the evening of Independence Day.

MAY DAY

May Day, on May 1, is another holiday celebrated with much enthusiasm in Finland. There are parades, speeches, fairs, and concerts to mark the occasion. Factories that pride themselves on running their operations all year round are closed on two days of the year: Christmas and May Day. May 1 is also seen as a celebration of the coming of spring.

STUDENTS' DAY

This celebration begins on the evening of May Day, when students in Helsinki gather at the fountain of a mermaid near the harbor. At midnight, a student climbs the statue to place a student's cap on its head. The cap is white with a black visor. The festivities continue into the next day with processions and more merrymaking.

NEW YEAR'S EVE

On New Year's Eve a small piece of lead is melted and then thrown into a bucket of water and left to harden. The shape that it forms is purported to tell the future: lumps and bulges signify money coming in, black spots are a sign of sadness, while a boat shape predicts travel.

"This nation's roots are deep and firm and mountain strong. Its people love this land alone, its laws and language that they own, the ancient songs that hold and keep their fathers' mem'ries green."

—Eino Leino, "This Nation on a Rock"

CALENDAR OF PUBLIC HOLIDAYS

New Year's Day	January 1
Epiphany	January 6
Good Friday	April
Easter	April
May Day	May 1
Ascension Day	May
Whitsun	May
Midsummer's Day	third weekend in June
All Saints' Day	November
Independence Day	December 6
Christmas Day	December 25
Boxing Day/St. Stephen's Day	December 26

FOOD

TYPICAL FINNISH CUISINE is a blend of Eastern, or Russian, and Western, or Swedish, influences, with a bit of the Scandinavian and Baltic thrown in. It tends to change seasonally, reaping the generous bounty of mother nature. Indeed, the country's forests, rivers, and lakes are the richest sources of food. Geographical location also plays a part, giving rise to regional specialties.

Recipes are traditional, passed down from one generation to another, and flavors are kept as natural as possible. Finnish food is thus rather simple but wholesome and prepared from the freshest ingredients. Meals are eaten with rye bread on the side.

What is truly astonishing is the variety of dishes available each season. As a nation of thousands of lakes, it is not surprising that much of the local cuisine revolves around fish. During the summer, salmon, Baltic herring, and whitefish are available all over the country. There is also crayfish from the end of July through September.

While fish, especially salmon, is enjoyed grilled or smoked, the Finns prefer to eat freshly boiled crayfish, which tastes and looks like a miniature version of the American lobster. Other times of the year, there are other kinds of freshwater fish, like rainbow trout, pike, Finnish whitefish, perch, grayling, and zander.

Summer also yields a great variety of vegetables and berries. A favorite vegetable dish is made of new potatoes that are freshly dug up in June. They are boiled in dill and served with butter and raw herring. A wide range of berries can be found, which are often made into pastries to satisfy the Finnish sweet tooth. A visitor to the country should not miss the

Above: **Fresh produce is available from vegetable markets like this one in Helsinki.**

Opposite: **A vendor sells fresh herring from her boat anchored at Market Square in Helsinki.**

Sorbet with cloudberries and strawberries, a typical Finnish dessert that makes good use of the many fresh fruits available in the country.

blueberry pie or wild strawberries with cream, or the many liqueurs made from berries such as arctic bramberries and cloudberries.

Autumn is a time for wild mushrooms such as chanterelles and morels, which are often made into a delicious, light, creamy soup known as *korvasienikeitto* ("KORR-va-sie-ni-KAY-ee-toh"). It is also the hunting season for game, of which there is plenty in Finland: elk, hare, black grouse, capercaillie, and ptarmigan.

In winter, body-warming soups and pies are popular, as well as turnips and rutabagas, two winter roots. Fish is also featured in soups, and *lohikeitto* ("LOH-i-KAY-ee-toh," or salmon soup) with potatoes, dill, and milk is especially tasty. A very special fish dish appearing on restaurant menus in February is *mäti* ("MUTT-ee-ya"), a roe from freshwater fish, dubbed Finnish caviar. Yellow or orange in color, the fine roe is exquisite when served with chopped onions and *smetana* ("SMAY-ta-na," or sour cream).

Oddly enough, it is not always easy to find typical Finnish food outside private homes. Helsinki, for instance, has many excellent Russian restaurants, while menus in most restaurants tend to be international. Meat dishes, for instance, are cooked French-style, unless it is game or reindeer. However, fish, soups, and desserts are usually in the Finnish tradition.

An alternative to eating out in a restaurant would be to visit one of the many small and cozy outdoor cafes for a light meal. Most people drop by to have coffee with pastries or the quintessential Finnish *pulla* ("POO-lah"), a sweet bread with cardamom that is sprinkled with sugar.

A smorgasbord offering a variety of salads and Finnish food.

SMORGASBORD

Smorgasbord is not exactly Finnish in origin, as it was the Swedes who made it famous. Still, a foreigner staying in a tourist hotel in Finland will often come across smorgasbord served for breakfast or lunch. It includes a wide array of dishes ranging from smoked salmon and salami to reindeer meat, cheeses, and salads. It is a great menu choice as the buffet offers a variety of different Finnish dishes to taste.

CHRISTMAS FARE

Christmas is a time for feasting. The celebration begins on December 24 and starts with breakfast, when a traditional rice pudding is eaten. An almond is hidden in the pudding, and whoever bites into it has to "pay" a penalty such as singing a song or reciting a poem. Then follows the busiest time of the year—last-minute shopping, decorating the Christmas tree, and wrapping the presents.

In the early evening, many people go to the cemetery to spare a thought for their departed ones. They pray and light candles on family graves. Then it is time to enjoy a sauna before sitting down to feast.

A glass of warming grogg or spiced mulled wine is first served as an aperitif to get the party

going. The meal itself begins with lightly salted salmon, herring prepared in various ways, and other types of cold hors d'oeuvres. The main dish is glazed ham cooked overnight in a slow oven. It is accompanied by other oven-baked dishes made from carrots, potatoes, rutabagas, and liver, and slices of a Christmas bread that is sweet and spicy. A home-brewed ale is traditionally drunk at Christmas. Dessert may be prune parfait or pies made from berries. The rest of the evening is spent at home, chatting and drinking in front of a fire.

Those who choose to enjoy a sauna at this time usually follow it with a meal of fish, ham, and rice pudding. In both the city and countryside, animals and birds are given extra food.

Christmas Day starts early when Finnish families go to church. Then it is time for more feasting on rich Christmas pies such as *joulutorttu* ("YO-loo-TORR-too," or tiny pastries stuffed with pulped prunes), gingerbread, date, and fruit cake. Boxing Day on December 26 is reserved for visiting friends and relatives and finishing the Christmas food. A dance in the evening usually marks the end of the festive season.

REGIONAL SPECIALTIES

Karelia in the east and Lapland in the north boast the greatest variety of regional specialties in Finland. *Karjalanpaisti* ("KAR-ee-larn-PA-I-ees-tee") is a Karelian meat casserole, a hearty blend of beef, pork, and mutton, eaten traditionally in winter.

Karjalan piirakat ("KAR-ee-larn PEE-rak-ka") are Karelian pastries made of rye dough that are filled with rice or mashed potatoes and served hot with hard-boiled eggs and butter. Also from eastern Finland, particularly Kuopio, is *kalakukko* ("KA-LA-koo-koh"), which is fish and bacon baked inside a crust of rye bread.

Reindeer is typically Finnish and it is eaten in many forms, grilled as steaks or chops, or cooked in stews. In Lapland, you will find *poronpaisti* ("POH-ron-PA-I-stee"), a reindeer roast, and *poronkäristys* ("POH-ron-KA-ri-stees"), which are thin strips of smoked reindeer meat. *Mustamakkara* ("MUST-ah-MAH-ka-ra") is grilled black pudding, a Tampere specialty, served with red whortleberries.

A selection of Finnish liqueurs.

DRINKS

The Finns enjoy drinking and have all sorts of alcoholic concoctions made with locally available ingredients. Finland is noted for its berry liqueurs and grain spirits. The liqueurs are fairly sweet and are usually made from wild berries. There is *lakkalikööri* ("LAK-ka-li-koo-ee-ree") made from golden yellow cloudberries that grow on arctic and subarctic bogs. The rich, strong-flavored liqueur is reputedly full of vitamin C.

Another strong berry liqueur is *puolukkalikööri* ("POO-loo-kah-LEE-koo-ee-ree"), made from red whortleberries or cowberries. The rare arctic brambleberry, which looks like a wild strawberry, makes a sweet but delicate liqueur called *mesimarjalikööri* ("MES-see-mar-ya-lee-koo-ee-ree").

The best-known Finnish grain spirit is Finlandia vodka, which comes in an iced bottle seen in most international duty-free shops. However, the connoisseurs' choice seems to be *Koskenkorva-Viina* ("KOS-ken-KOR-va-VEE-na"), a 38% vodka distilled from wheat.

The Finns have their own version of champagne, actually a sparkling wine fermented from white currants and gooseberries. Beer is light, similar to a lager. There are different varieties: alcohol-free or low-alcohol that are sold in supermarkets, and strong beer available only from the Alko liquor monopoly stores. A home-made, low-alcohol beer brewed from a mixture of water, malt, sugar, and yeast is *kotikalja* ("KO-tee-CAR-lee-ya"), a must on every rural buffet table.

KARELIAN STEW

This is a local delicacy of Karelia in eastern Finland and a traditional favorite.

Ingredients
1 lb (500 g) beef
$^{1}/_{2}$ lb (250 g) mutton
$^{1}/_{2}$ lb (250 g) pork
one calf kidney
$^{1}/_{2}$ lb (250 g) liver
one onion (optional)
$^{1}/_{8}$–$^{1}/_{4}$ tsp whole allspice
1 tbsp salt
water

Method
1. Trim the meat and cut into chunky pieces.
2. Place the meat and spices in layers in an oven-proof casserole with the pork on top.
3. Add enough water to cover the meat.
4. Bake in a hot oven at about 475°F (225°C), first without a lid, to brown the meat. Then cover and lower the oven temperature to 350°F (175°C). Bake for two to three hours.

BREAD AND COFFEE

Bread is a staple in every Finnish home. In the east, it is baked weekly. In the west, some rural households still bake their bread twice a year in enormous ovens. They string up their loaves through a hole in the middle and hang them on a pole to dry. Each day, a loaf is taken down and soaked in milk before being consumed. In the urban towns, there are bakeries where fresh bread can be bought daily. Bread is usually consumed at breakfast, together with cereal, oat porridge, and sausages. Sandwiches may be eaten at other times when there is a need for a quick meal.

The Finns are avid coffee drinkers, drinking more coffee per capita than any other people in the world. Coffee is served in the morning, afternoon, and evening. Drinking coffee is an event that should not be rushed. One sits with a friend or business associate and sips leisurely. Sandwiches and pastries are usually served.

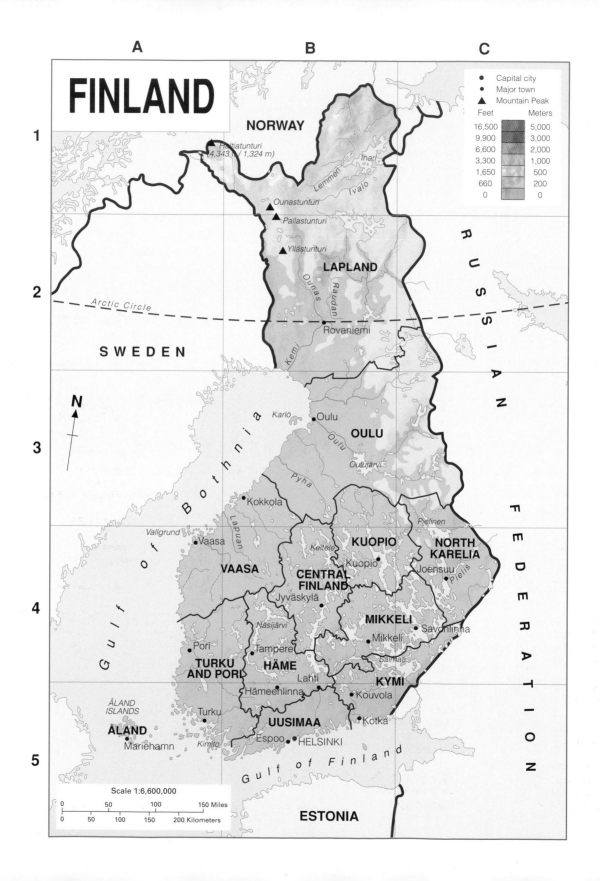

FINLAND

A   **B**   **C**

NORWAY

1

Haltiatunturi
(4,343 ft / 1,324 m)

Inari

Lemmen

Ivalo

▲ *Ounastunturi*

▲ *Pallastunturi*

▲ *Yllästunturi*

LAPLAND

Ounas

Raudan

2

Arctic Circle

S W E D E N

Kemi

Rovaniemi

	Capital city
●	Major town
▲	Mountain Peak

Feet	Meters
16,500	5,000
9,900	3,000
6,600	2,000
3,300	1,000
1,650	500
660	200
0	0

R U S S I A N

3

N

Karlö

● Oulu

OULU

Oulu

Oulujärvi

Pyhä

● Kokkola

Pielinen

KUOPIO

NORTH KARELIA

Vallgrund

● Vaasa

VAASA

Lapuan

Keitele

● Kuopio

Joensuu ●

Pielis

F E D E R A T I O N

CENTRAL FINLAND

Jyväskylä ●

4

● Pori

Näsijärvi

● Tampere

TURKU AND PORI

HÄME

Lahti ●

Hämeenlinna ●

MIKKELI

● Mikkeli

Savonlinna ●

Saimaa

KYMI

● Kouvola

● Kotka

ÅLAND ISLANDS

● Turku

ÅLAND

UUSIMAA

● Espoo

● Mariehamn

Kimito

Espoo ● HELSINKI

5

Gulf of Finland

ESTONIA

Scale 1:6,600,000

0	50	100	150 Miles
0	50	100	150	200 Kilometers

Gulf of Bothnia

QUICK NOTES

OFFICIAL NAME
Republic of Finland

LAND AREA
130,559 square miles (338,147 square kilometers)

POPULATION
5,077,912 (1993 estimate)

OFFICIAL LANGUAGES
Finnish and Swedish

CAPITAL
Helsinki

PROVINCES
Lapland, Oulu, Vaasa, Central Finland, Kuopio, North Karelia, Turku and Pori, Hame, Mikkeli, Åland Islands, Kymi, and Uusimaa

MAJOR CITIES
Espoo, Tampere, Turku, Vantaa, Oulu, Kuopio, and Rovaniemi

NATIONAL FLAG
Blue cross on a white background, symbolizing the blue color of the country's lakes and the white snow of its winters

MAJOR LAKES
Saimaa, Pielinen, and Päijänne. Finland is a land of lakes—about 188,000 connected to one another by a network of rivers

HIGHEST POINT
Haltiatunturi: 4,343 feet (1,324 meters)

MAJOR RELIGION
Lutheranism

CURRENCY
The Finnish *markka* (FIM), which is divided into 100 pennies (p)
US$1 = FIM 4.26

MAIN EXPORTS
Engineering and metal products, paper and pulp, chemicals, wood products, and textiles

IMPORTANT HOLIDAYS
New Year's Day, January 1
Easter (Good Friday to Easter Monday)
Midsummer's Day, third weekend in June
Independence Day, December 6
Christmas, December 25
Boxing Day/St. Stephen's Day, Dec. 26

PRESIDENTS OF FINLAND

K. J. Ståhlberg	1919-1925
Lauri Kr Relander	1925-1931
P.E. Svinhufvud	1931-1937
Kyosti Kallio	1937-1940
Risto Ryti	1940-1944
C.G. Mannerheim	1944-1946
J.K. Paasikivi	1946-1956
Urho Kekkonen	1956-1981
Mauno Koivisto	1982-1995
Martti Ahtisaari	1994-

GLOSSARY

ei ("ay")
No.

eskers
Long, level ridges of sand and rock left behind when glaciers melt and recede.

Jouli ("YO-lo")
The Christmas holiday.

Juhannus ("yu-HAHN-os")
Midsummer celebration held on June 23, usually highlighted by a bonfire.

kaamos ("KAAH-mos")
"Sunless days" in the arctic region when the sun never rises. This season lasts nearly six months.

kantele ("KAHN-tay-leh")
An ancient harp-like instrument traditionally used to accompany rune singers.

kiitos ("KEEH-tos")
Thank you.

kylla ("KOO-la")
Yes.

korvasienkeitto ("KORR-va-sie-ni-KAY-ee-toh")
A light, creamy soup.

lohikeitto ("LOH-i-KAY-ee-toh")
A salmon soup.

matia ("MUTT-ee-ya")
Roe from a freshwater fish.

nakemlin ("NA-kem-een")
Goodbye.

olkaa hyva ("all-KAA hoo-va")
Please.

pesapallo ("pay-SA-PARL-lo")
A type of baseball game.

poronpaisti ("POH-ron-PA-I-ees-tee")
A reindeer roast.

pulla ("POO-lah")
Sweet bread flavored with cardamon that is sprinkled with sugar..

saari ("SAAH-ri")
Island.

smetana ("SMAY-ta-na")
Sour cream.

Tapaninpäivä ("TAH-pa-neen-PAI-va")
Boxing Day, on December 26.

Ukko ("OO-ko")
The ancient Finnish god of thunder and lightning.

ukkonen ("OO-ko-nen")
Thunder.

BIBLIOGRAPHY

The Fish of Gold and Other Finnish Folk Tales. Iowa City: Penfield Press, 1990.

Lander, Patricia and Charbonneau, Claudette. *The Land and People of Finland.* New York: J.B. Lippincott, 1990.

Finland—in Pictures. Minneapolis: Lerner Publications Company, 1991.

Rajanen. *Of Finnish Ways.* New York: HarperCollins, 1990.

Singleton, Frederick B. *A Short History of Finland.* New York: Cambridge University Press, 1990.

Solsten, Eric and Meditz, S.W, eds. *Finland: A Country Study,* 2nd edition. Washington: U.S. Government Printing Office, 1991.

INDEX

INDEX

INDEX

PICTURE CREDITS